On Learning and Knowledge

Also by J. Krishnamurti

On Learning and Knowledge

J. Krishnamurti

HarperSanFrancisco
A Division of HarperCollins*Publishers*

For additional information, write to:
Krishnamurti Foundation Trust, Ltd.
Brockwood Park, Bramdean, Hampshire, England SO24 0LQ

or

Krishnamurti Foundation of America
P.O. Box 1560
Ojai, CA 93024-1560, United States

Sources and acknowledgments can be found on page 151.

Series editor: Mary Cadogan

Associate editors: Ray McCoy and David Skitt

FIRST EDITION

Library of Congress Cataloging-in-Publication Data

Krishnamurti, J. (Jiddu) 1895–1986

On learning and knowledge / J. Krishnamurti. — 1st ed.

p. cm.

ISBN 0-06-251011-8 (pbk. : alk. paper)

1. Conduct of life. 2. Self-realization. 3. Knowledge, Theory of. I. Title.

B5134.K753055 1994

121—dc20
93-44276
CIP

94 95 96 97 98 99 ❖ CWI 10 9 8 7 6 5 4 3 2 1

This edition is printed on acid-free paper that meets the American National
Standards Institute Z39.48 Standard.

The ascent of man does not lie in accumulated knowledge. . . . Scientists and others have said man can only evolve by having more and more knowledge, climbing, ascending. But knowledge is always the past; and if there is no freedom from the past, his ascent will be always limited. It will always be confined to a particular pattern. We are saying there is a different way of learning, which is to see comprehensively, wholly, holistically the whole movement of knowledge. Knowledge is necessary; otherwise you couldn't live, but the very understanding of its limitation is to have insight into its whole movement. We have taken knowledge as natural, and live with knowledge, and go on functioning with knowledge for the rest of our life, but we have never asked what knowledge itself is, and what its relationship is to freedom, what its relationship is to what is actually happening. We have taken all this for granted. That's part of our education and conditioning.

Ojai, 15 April 1979

Contents

Foreword

JIDDU KRISHNAMURTI was born in India in 1895 and, at the age of thirteen, was taken up by the Theosophical Society, which considered him to be the vehicle for the 'world teacher' whose advent it had been proclaiming. Krishnamurti was soon to emerge as a powerful, uncompromising, and unclassifiable teacher, whose talks and writings were not linked to any specific religion and were of neither the East nor the West but for the whole world. Firmly repudiating the messianic image, in 1929 he dramatically dissolved the large and monied organization that had been built around him and declared truth to be 'a pathless land', which could not be approached by any formalized religion, philosophy, or sect.

For the rest of his life Krishnamurti insistently rejected the guru status that others tried to foist upon him. He continued to attract large audiences throughout the world but claimed no authority, wanted no disciples, and spoke always as one individual to another. At the core of his teaching was the realization that fundamental changes in society can be brought about only by a transformation of individual consciousness. The need for self-knowledge and understanding of the restrictive, separative influences of religious and nationalistic conditionings was constantly stressed. Krishnamurti pointed always to the urgent need for openness, for that 'vast space in the brain in which there is unimaginable energy'. This seems to have been the wellspring of his own creativity and the key to his catalytic impact on such a wide variety of people.

Krishnamurti continued to speak all over the world until he died in 1986 at the age of ninety. His talks and dialogues, journals and letters have been preserved in over sixty books and hundreds of recordings. From that vast body of teachings this series of theme books has been compiled. Each book focuses on an issue that has particular relevance to and urgency in our daily lives.

Madras, 22 October 1958

OUR PROBLEM IS the mind, the mind which is conditioned, which is shaped, which is the plaything of every influence, every culture, the mind which is the result of the past, burdened with innumerable memories, experiences. How is such a mind to free itself from all this and be a total individual? I say it is possible only when there is serious, earnest study of oneself—the self not being the *atman* or some so-called *higher self*, because those again are just words. I am talking of the self of everyday existence, the self that gets angry, the self that is ambitious, that gets hurt, that wants to be seen, that is very keen, that says, 'I must be secure', 'I must consider my position', and so on. That is the only self we have. The higher self, the super-atman, is only an ideology, a concept, an unreality; and it is no good going after unreality, for that leads to delusion. I know all the sacred books talk about the super-atman, whatever that is, and for the man who is caught in the daily self it is a marvellous escape. The more he speculates, the more he writes about it, the more religious he thinks he is. But I say that if you can go into the self that we all know, the self of everyday movement, then through that self-knowledge, through careful analysis, careful observation, you will find that you are capable of breaking away from all influences that condition thought.

Another thing is that thought, by the very thinking process, conditions itself. Is it not so? Whatever thought you have affects the mind. Whether the thought is good or bad, ugly or beautiful, subtle or cunning—whatever thought it be, it shapes the mind. So what is thinking? Thinking, surely, is the reaction of what you know. Knowledge reacts, and we call it thinking. Please observe it. If you are alert, aware of your own process of thinking, you will see that whatever you think has already shaped the mind; and a mind that is shaped by thought has ceased to be free, and therefore it is not a mind that is individual.

So self-knowledge is not a process of the continuity of thinking but the diminishing, the ending of thinking. But you cannot end thinking by any trick, by denial, by control, by discipline. If you do, you are still caught in the field of thought. Thinking can only come to an end when you know the total content of the thinker, and so one begins to see how important it is to have self-knowledge. Most of us are satisfied with superficial self-knowledge, with scratching on the surface, the ordinary ABC of psychology. It is no good to read a few books on psychology, scratch a little, and say you know. That is merely applying to the mind what you have learned. Therefore you must begin to ask what learning is. Do you see the relationship between self-knowledge and learning? A mind that has self-knowledge is learning, whereas a mind that merely applies acquired knowledge to itself and thinks it is self-knowledge is merely accumulating. A mind that accumulates can never learn. Please observe. Do you ever learn? Have you found out yet whether you learn anything, or whether you just accumulate information?

Without self-knowledge there is no individual. You read that statement—what is your reaction to it? Don't you say, 'What do you mean by that?' That is, you say, 'Explain, and I will either agree or disagree with you', and you say afterwards that you have learned something. But is that learning? Is learning a matter of agreement or disagreement? Can you not inquire into that statement without agreement or disagreement? Surely you want to find out if that statement is false or true, not whether you agree or disagree. No one cares if you agree or disagree, but if you find out for yourself whether that statement has truth in it or not, then you are actually beginning to see, to learn.

So a mind that agrees or disagrees, that comes to a conclusion, is not capable of learning. A specialized mind is never a creative mind. The mind that has accumulated, that is steeped in knowledge, is incapable of learning. To learn there must be a freshness; there must be a mind that says, 'I do not know, but I am willing to learn. Show me'. And if there is no one to show, it begins to inquire of itself. It does not start from a fixed point and move to another fixed point. That is what we do, isn't it? We come to a conclusion, and from that fixed point we think more and move to another conclusion. And this process we call learning. But if you observe, you will see that you are tied to a post and merely move to another post. That is not learning at all. Learning demands a mind that is willing to learn but not in order to add to itself. Because the moment you are engaged in adding to yourself, you have ceased to learn. So self-knowledge is not a process of addition. What you are learning is about the self, about the ways of the mind. You are learning of its cunningness, its subtleties, its motives, its extraordinary capacities, its depth, its vastness. And to learn you must come with enormous humility. A man who has accumulated knowledge can never know humility. He may talk about humility, he may quote words about humility, but he has no sense of humility. The man who learns is essentially humble.

So we have this problem of bringing about the true individual. Such an individual cannot be created except through self-knowledge, and you have to learn about the self. There cannot be any condemnation of what you find, and there cannot be any identification with what you find, for any identification, justification, or condemnation is the result of accumulation, and therefore you cease to learn. Please see the importance of this. It may sound very contradictory, but it is not. If you will observe, you will see how necessary it is to learn, and to learn there must be a sense of complete humility, and there is no humility if there is condemnation of what you see in yourself. Similarly, if you see something good and identify yourself with that, then you cease to learn. So a mind that is capable of learning is the true individual mind, not the mind that has accumulated. At present we are all the time adding to our accumulations.

For instance, have you ever examined what experience is? Observe; do not just listen to me but watch your mind and go into it as I am talking. When you say, 'I have had an experience', what do you mean by that? *Experience* means—does it not?—a sensation, a reaction that is recognizable. I recognize that I am having a pleasurable experience or a painful one. I recognize it because I have had a similar experience before. So the previous experiences condition the present experience. It is not a fresh experience. If it is a new experience, it is immediately recognized and translated and put into the old. So every experience conditions the mind, because all experience is recognized by means of previous experience. So experience is never a liberating factor.

While the whole world is developing technicians, specialists, with every thought shaped and conditioned, there is no possibility of anyone being an individual. The possibility of being an individual comes only when you begin to understand and learn about yourself, not through books, because the self—what you are—cannot be understood through someone else. You have to observe it yourself, and you can observe it with clarity, strength, and purposive directiveness only in relationship. The way you behave, the way you talk, how you look at a flower, a tree, the way you speak to a servant, the movement of your hands, your eyes, everything will show, if you are at all aware, how your mind works, and the mind is the self. It can invent the super-self—or it can invent hell—but it is still the mind.

Unless the mind understands itself, there is no freedom. Freedom cannot come by accumulation. You have to learn what an extraordinary thing the mind is. It is the most marvellous thing we have, but we don't know how to use it. We only use it at certain levels, specialized self-centred levels. It is a magnificent instrument, a living thing of which we still know very little. We only know the superficial stretches, the thin layers of consciousness, but we do not know the total being of the mind, the extraordinary depths. And you cannot know it merely by speculating about it. You can only learn about it, and to learn you must give total attention. Attention is different from concentration. Concentration merely narrows the mind, but attention is a state in which everything is.

So what is of importance for a religious man is not the repetition of what he has learned from books or the experiences that his conditioning has projected but being concerned with the understanding of himself without any delusion, without any warping, without any twist—to see things in himself as they are. And to see things as they actually are is an enormous task. I do not know if you have ever done it. I do not know if you have ever observed anything without colouring it, without twisting it, without naming it. I suggest you try to look at what you call greed, or envy, and see how difficult it is to look at it, because the very words *greed, envy*, carry with them a condemnatory significance. You may be a greedy man, an ambitious man, but to look at the feeling, the sensation of ambition without condemning it, just to look at it, requires, as you will see, extraordinary capacity.

All this is a part of self-knowledge, and without self-knowledge, do what you will, reform, have every kind of revolution, super-leaders, super-politicians, you will never create a world in which the individual becomes a total being and so can influence society. So if you are interested in this, then we will go into it very, very seriously. But if you only want to go into it superficially, it is much better not to do so. It is far better to have a few people who are really serious than many who are followers. What is necessary is earnestness, an earnest mind that begins to inquire within itself. Such a mind will find for itself that which is real.

Bombay, 24 February 1957

As LIFE IS so complicated, it seems to me that one must approach it with great simplicity. Life is a vast complex of struggle, of misery, of passing joys, and, perhaps for some, the pleasurable continuity of a satisfaction they have known. Confronted with this extraordinarily intricate process that we call existence, surely we must approach it very simply; because it is the simple mind that really understands the problem, not the sophisticated mind, not the mind that is burdened with knowledge. If we want to understand something very complex, we must approach it very simply, and therein lies our difficulty—because we always approach our problems with assertions, with assumptions or conclusions, and so we are never free to approach them with the humility they demand.

Mere verbal or intellectual listening has no significance when we are confronted with immense problems. So let us try to listen, for the time being at least, not just on the verbal level, or with certain conclusions at which the mind may have arrived, but with a sense of humility so that you and I can explore together this whole problem of knowledge.

The undoing of knowledge is the fundamental revolution; the undoing of knowledge is the beginning of humility. Only the mind that is humble can understand what is true and what is false and is therefore capable of eschewing the false and pursuing that which is true. But most of us approach life with knowledge, knowledge being what we have learned, what we have been taught, and what we have gathered in the incidents and accidents of life. This knowledge becomes our background, our conditioning. It shapes our thoughts; it makes us conform to the pattern of what has been. If we would understand anything, we must approach it with humility; and it is knowledge that makes us un-humble. Have you noticed that when you know, you have ceased to examine what is? When you already know, you are not living at all. Only the mind that is undoing what it has gathered, that is actually and not merely intellectually dissipating what it has known, is capable of understanding. And for most of us, knowledge becomes the authority, the guide that keeps us within the sanctuary of society, within the frontiers of respectability. Knowledge is the centre from which we judge, evaluate, from which we condemn, accept, or reject.

Is it possible for the mind to free itself from knowledge? Can that self-centre, which is essentially the accumulation of knowledge, be dissolved, so that the mind is really humble, innocent, and therefore capable of perceiving what is truth?

After all, what is it that we know? We know only facts, or what we have been taught about facts. When I examine and ask myself, 'What is it that I really know?' I see that I actually know only what has been taught me, a technique, a profession, plus the information that I have acquired in the everyday relationship of challenge and response. Apart from that, what do I know? What do you know? What we know is obviously what we have been taught or what we have gathered from books and from environmental influences. This accumulation of what we have acquired or been taught reacts to the environment, thereby further strengthening the background of what we call knowledge.

So can the mind, which has been put together through knowledge, undo what it has gathered and thereby remove authority altogether? It is the authority of knowledge that gives us arrogance, vanity, and there is humility only when that authority is removed, not theoretically but actually, so that we can approach this whole complex process of existence with a mind that does not know. Is it possible for the mind to free itself from that which it has known?

We can see that there is a great deal of tyranny in the world, and that tyranny is spreading; there is compulsion, there is misery, both physically and inwardly, and the constant threat of war; and with such a world there must obviously be some kind of radical change in our thinking. But most of us regard action as more important than thought; we want to know what to do about all these complex problems, and we are more concerned with right action than with the process of thinking that will produce right action.

Now the process of thinking obviously cannot be made new as long as one starts by thinking from any assumption, from any conclusion. So I must ask myself, as you must ask yourself, whether it is possible for the mind to undo the knowledge it has gathered; because knowledge becomes authority, which produces arrogance, and with that arrogance and vanity we consciously or unconsciously look at life, and therefore we never approach anything with humility.

I know because I have learned, I have experienced, I have gathered, or I guide my thought and activity in terms of some ideology to which I conform. So gradually I build up this whole process of authority in myself, the authority of the experiencer, of the one who knows. And my problem is: can I, who have gathered so much knowledge, who have learned so much, who have had so many experiences, undo all that? Because there is no possibility of a radical change without the undoing of knowledge. The very undoing of knowledge is the beginning of such a change, is it not?

What do we mean by *change?* Is change merely a movement from the knowledge I have accumulated to other fields of knowing, to new assumptions and ideologies projected from the past? This is generally what we mean by *change*, is it not? When I say I must change, I think in terms of changing to something I already know. When I say I must be good, I have an idea, a formulation, a concept of what it is to be good. But that is not the flowering of goodness. The flowering of goodness comes only when I understand the process and the accumulation of knowledge, and in the undoing of what I know. Then there is the possibility of a revolution, a radical change. But merely to move from the known to the known is no change at all.

I hope I am making myself clear, because you and I do need to change radically, in a tremendous, revolutionary way. It is an obvious fact that we cannot go on as we are. The appalling things that are taking place in the world demand an approach to all these problems from a totally different point of view, with a totally different heart and mind. That is why I must understand how to bring about in myself this radical change. And I see that I can change only when I am undoing what I have known. The disentangling of the mind from knowledge is in itself a radical change, because then the mind is humble, and that very humility brings about an action that is totally new. As long as the mind is acquiring, comparing, thinking in terms of 'the more', it is obviously incapable of action that is new. And can I, who am envious, acquisitive, change completely, so that my mind is no longer acquiring, comparing, competing? To put it differently, can my mind empty itself and in that very process of emptying itself discover the action that is new?

So is it possible to bring about a fundamental change that is not the outcome of an action of will, that is not merely the result of influence, pressure? Change based on influence, pressure, on an action of will, is no change at all. That is obvious if you go into it. And if I feel the necessity of a complete, radical change within myself, I must surely inquire into the process of knowledge, which forms the centre from which all experience takes place. There is a centre in each one of us that is the result of experience, of knowledge, of memory, and according to that centre we act, we 'change', and the very undoing of that centre, the very dissolution of that 'me', of that self, of that process of accumulation, brings about a radical change. But that demands the hard work that is involved in self-knowledge.

I must know myself as I am, not as I think I should be. I must know myself as the centre from which I am acting, from which I am thinking, the centre that is made up of accumulated knowledge, of assumptions, of past experience, all of which are preventing an inward revolution, a radical transformation of myself. And as we have so many complexities in the world at the present time, with so many superficial changes going on, it is necessary that there should be this radical change in the individual, for it is only the individual, and not the collective, that can bring about a new world.

Looking at all this, is it possible for you and me as two individuals to change, not superficially but radically, so that there is the dissolution of that centre from which all vanity, all sense of authority springs, that centre that actively accumulates, that centre that is made up of knowledge, experience, memory?

This is a question that cannot be answered verbally. I put it only in order to awaken your thinking, your inquiry, so that you will start on the journey alone. Because you cannot start on this journey with the help of another; you cannot have a guru to tell you what to do, what to seek. If you are told, then you are no longer on this journey. But can you not start on this journey of inquiry alone, without the accumulation of knowledge that prevents further inquiry? In order to inquire, the mind must be free of knowledge. If there is any pressure behind the inquiry, then the inquiry is not straight, it becomes crooked, and that is why it is so essential to have a mind that is really humble, a mind that says, 'I do not know; I will inquire', and that never gathers in the process of inquiring. The moment you gather, you have a centre, and that centre always influences your inquiry.

So can the mind inquire without accumulating, without gathering, without emphasizing the centre through the authority of knowledge? And if it can, then what is the state of such a mind? What is the state of the mind that is really inquiring? Surely, its state is that of emptiness.

I do not know if you have ever experienced what it is to be completely alone, without any pressure, without any motive or influence, without the idea of the past and the future. To be completely alone is entirely different from loneliness. There is loneliness when the centre of accumulation feels cut off in its relations with another. I am not talking of that feeling of loneliness. I am talking of the aloneness in which the mind is not contaminated, because it has understood the process of contamination, which is accumulation. And when the mind is totally alone because through self-knowledge it has understood the centre of accumulation, then you will find that, being empty, uninfluenced, the mind is capable of action that is not related to ambition, to envy, or to any of the conflicts that we know. Such a mind, being indifferent in the sense that it is not seeking a result, is capable of living with compassion. But such a state of mind is not to be acquired; it is not to be developed. It comes into being through self-knowledge, through knowing yourself—not some enormous, greater self, but the little self that is envious, greedy, petty, angry, vicious. What is necessary is to know the whole of that mind that is your little self. To go very far, you must begin very near, and the near is you, the 'you' that you must understand. And as you begin to understand, you will see that there is a dissolution of knowledge, so that the mind becomes totally alert, aware, empty, without that centre. And only such a mind is capable of perceiving that which is truth.

The Learned or the Wise?
From Commentaries on Living
First Series

THE RAINS HAD washed away the dust and heat of many months, and the leaves were sparklingly clean, with new leaves beginning to show. All through the night the frogs filled the air with their deep croaking; they would take a rest and start again. The river was swift-flowing, and there was softness in the air. The rains were not over by any means. Dark clouds were gathering, and the sun was hidden. The earth, the trees, and the whole of nature seemed to be waiting for another purification. The road was dark brown, and the children were playing in the puddles; they were making mud-pies or building castles and houses with surrounding walls. There was joy in the air after months of heat, and green grass was beginning to cover the earth. Everything was renewing itself.

This renewal is innocence.

The man considered himself vastly learned, and to him knowledge was the very essence of life. Life without knowledge was worse than death. His knowledge was not about one or two things but covered a great many phases of life; he could talk with assurance about the atom and communism, about astronomy and the yearly flow of water in the river, about diet and over-population.

He was strangely proud of his knowledge, and, like a clever show-man, he brought it to impress; it made the others silent and respectful. How frightened we are of knowledge; what awesome respect we show to the knower! His English was sometimes rather difficult to understand. He had never been outside of his own country, but he had books from other countries. He was addicted to knowledge as another might be to drink or to some other appetite.

'What is wisdom, if it is not knowledge? Why do you say that one must suppress all knowledge? Is not knowledge essential? Without knowledge, where would we be? We would still be as the primitives, knowing nothing of the extraordinary world we live in. Without knowledge, existence at any level would be impossible. Why are you so insistent in saying that knowledge is an impediment to understanding?'

Knowledge is conditioning. Knowledge does not give freedom. One may know how to build an aeroplane and fly to the other end of the world in a few hours, but this is not freedom. Knowledge is not the creative factor, for knowledge is continuous, and that which has continuity can never lead to the implicit, the imponderable, the unknown. Knowledge is a hindrance to the open, to the unknown. The unknown can never be clothed in the known; the known is always moving to the past; the past is ever overshadowing the present, the unknown. Without freedom, without the open mind, there can be no understanding. Understanding does not come with knowledge. In the interval between words, between thoughts, comes understanding. This interval is silence unbroken by knowledge; it is the open, the imponderable, the implicit.

'Is not knowledge useful, essential? Without knowledge, how can there be discovery?'

Discovery takes place not when the mind is crowded with knowledge but when knowledge is absent; only then are there stillness and space, and in this state understanding or discovery comes into being. Knowledge is undoubtedly useful at one level, but at another it is positively harmful. When knowledge is used as a means of self-aggrandizement, to puff oneself up, then it is mischievous, breeding separation and enmity. Self-expansion is disintegration, whether in the name of God, of the State, or of an ideology. Knowledge at one level, though conditioning, is necessary: language, technique, and so on. This conditioning is a safeguard, an essential for outer living; but when this conditioning is used psychologically, when knowledge becomes a means of psychological comfort, gratification, then it inevitably breeds conflict and confusion. Besides, what do we mean by knowing? What actually do you know?

'I know about a great many things.'

You mean you have lots of information, data about many things. You have gathered certain facts, and then what? Does information about the disaster of war prevent wars? You have, I am sure, plenty of data about the effects of anger and violence within oneself and in society, but has this information put an end to hate and antagonism?

'Knowledge about the effects of war may not put an immediate end to wars, but it will eventually bring about peace. People must be educated; they must be shown the effects of war, of conflict.'

People are yourself and another. You have this vast information, and are you any less ambitious, less violent, less self-centred? Because you have studied revolutions, the history of inequality, are you free from feeling superior, giving importance to yourself? Because you have extensive knowledge of the world's miseries and disasters, do you love? Besides, what is it that we know, of what have we knowledge?

'Knowledge is experience accumulated through the ages. In one form it is tradition, and in another it is instinct, both conscious and unconscious. The hidden memories and experiences, whether handed down or acquired, act as a guide and shape our action; these memories, both racial and individual, are essential, because they help and protect man. Would you do away with such knowledge?'

Action shaped and guided by fear is no action at all. Action that is the outcome of racial prejudices, fears, hopes, illusions, is conditioned; and all conditioning, as we said, only breeds further conflict and sorrow. You are conditioned as a brahmin in accordance with a tradition that has been going on for centuries; and you respond to stimuli, to social changes and conflicts, as a brahmin. You respond according to your conditioning, according to your past experiences, knowledge, so new experience only conditions further. Experience according to a belief, according to an ideology, is merely the continuation of that belief, the perpetuation of an idea. Such experience only strengthens belief. Idea separates, and your experience according to an idea, a pattern, makes you more separative. Experience as knowledge, as a psychological accumulation, only conditions, and experience is then another way of self-aggrandizement. Knowledge as experience at the psychological level is a hindrance to understanding.

'Do we experience according to our belief?'

That is obvious, is it not? You are conditioned by a particular society—which is yourself at a different level—to believe in God, in social divisions; and another is conditioned to believe that there is no God, to follow quite a different ideology. Both of you will experience according to your beliefs, but such experience is a hindrance to the unknown. Experience, knowledge, which is memory, is useful at certain levels; but experience as a means of strengthening the psychological 'me', the ego, only leads to illusion and sorrow. And what can we know if the mind is filled with experiences, memories, knowledge? Can there be experiencing if we know? Does not the known prevent experiencing? You may know the name of that flower, but do you thereby experience the flower? Experiencing comes first, and the naming only gives strength to the experience. The naming prevents further experiencing. For the state of experiencing, must there not be freedom from naming, from association, from the process of memory?

Knowledge is superficial, and can the superficial lead to the deep? Can the mind, which is the result of the known, of the past, ever go above and beyond its own projection? To discover, it must stop projecting. Without its projections, mind is not. Knowledge, the past, can project only that which is the known. The instrument of the known can never be the discoverer. The known must cease for discovery; the experience must cease for experiencing. Knowledge is a hindrance to understanding.

'What have we left if we are without knowledge, experience, memory? We are then nothing.'

Are you anything more than that now? When you say, 'Without knowledge we are nothing', you are merely making a verbal assertion without experiencing that state, are you not? When you make that statement, there is a sense of fear, the fear of being naked. Without these accretions you are nothing—which is the truth. And why not be that? Why all these pretensions and conceits? We have clothed this nothingness with fancies, with hopes, with various comforting ideas; but beneath these coverings we are nothing, not as some philosophical abstraction, but actually nothing. The experiencing of that nothingness is the beginning of wisdom.

How ashamed we are to say we do not know! We cover the fact of not knowing with words and information. Actually, you do not know your wife, your neighbour; how can you when you do not know yourself? You have a lot of information, conclusions, explanations about yourself, but you are not aware of that which is, the implicit. Explanations, conclusions, called *knowledge*, prevent the experiencing of what is. Without innocence, how can there be wisdom? Without the dying to the past, how can there be the renewing of innocence? Dying is from moment to moment. To die is not to accumulate; the experiencer must die to the experience. Without experience, without knowledge, the experiencer is not. To know is to be ignorant; not to know is the beginning of wisdom.

From Krishnamurti's Notebook, *Paris, September 1961*

September 6

THE SUN WAS just beginning to show through the clouds, early in the morning, and the daily roar of traffic had not yet begun; it was raining, and the sky was dull grey. On the little terrace the rain was beating down, and the breeze was fresh. Standing in the shelter, watching a stretch of the river and the autumnal leaves, there came that otherness, like a flash, and it remained for a while to be gone again. It's strange how very intense and actual it has become. It was as real as these roof-tops with hundreds of chimneys. In it there is a strange driving strength; because of its purity, it is strong, the strength of innocence that nothing can corrupt. And it was a benediction.

Knowledge is destructive to discovery. Knowledge is always in time, in the past; it can never bring freedom. But knowledge is necessary, to act, to think, and without action existence is not possible. But action, however wise, righteous, and noble, will not open the door to truth. There's no path to truth; it cannot be bought through any action or through any refinement of thought. Virtue is only order in a disordered world, and there must be virtue, which is a movement of non-conflict. But none of these

will open the door to that immensity. The totality of consciousness must empty itself of all its knowledge, action, and virtue—
not empty itself for a purpose, to gain, to realize, to become. It
must remain empty though functioning in the everyday world of
thought and action. Out of this emptiness, thought and action
must come. But this emptiness will not open the door. There
must be no door nor any attempt to reach. There must be no centre in this emptiness, for this emptiness has no measurement; it's
the centre that measures, weighs, calculates. This emptiness is
beyond time and space; it's beyond thought and feeling. It comes
as quietly, unobtrusively, as love; it has no beginning and end. It's
there unalterable and immeasurable.

September 8

Even the stars can be seen in this well-lighted town, and
there are other sounds than the roar of traffic—the cooing of pigeons and the chirping of sparrows; there are other smells than
the monoxide gases—the smell of autumn leaves and the scent of
flowers. There were a few stars in the sky and fleecy clouds early
this morning, and with them came that intense penetration into
the depth of the unknown. The brain was still, so still it could
hear the faintest noise, and, being still and so incapable of interfering, there was a movement that began from nowhere and went
on, through the brain, into unknown depth where the word lost its
meaning. It swept through the brain and went on beyond time
and space. One is not describing a fantasy, a dream, an illusion
but an actual fact that took place, but what took place is not the
word or the description. There was a burning energy, a bursting
immediate vitality, and with it came this penetrating movement.
It was like a tremendous wind, gathering strength and fury as it
rushed along, destroying, purifying, leaving a vast emptiness.
There was a complete awareness of the whole thing, and there
was great strength and beauty, not the strength and beauty that
are put together but of something that was completely pure and

incorruptible. It lasted by the watch ten minutes, but it was something incalculable.

The sun arose amidst a glory of clouds, fantastically alive and deep in colour. The roar of the town had not begun yet, and the pigeons and sparrows were out. How curiously shallow the brain is; however subtle and deep thought is, it's nevertheless born of shallowness. Thought is bound by time, and time is petty; it's this pettiness that perverts 'seeing'. Seeing is always instantaneous, as understanding, and the brain, which is put together by time, prevents and also perverts seeing. Time and thought are inseparable; put an end to one, you put an end to the other. Thought cannot be destroyed by will, for will is thought in action. Thought is one thing, and the centre from which thought arises is another. Thought is the word, and the word is the accumulation of memory, of experience. Without the word, is there thought? There's a movement that is not word and it is not of thought. This movement can be described by thought, but it is not of thought. This movement comes into being when the brain is still but active, and thought can never search out this movement.

Thought is memory and memory is accumulated responses and so thought is always conditioned, however much it may imagine it is free. Thought is mechanical, tied to the centre of its own knowledge. The distance thought covers depends on knowledge, and knowledge is always the remains of yesterday, of the movement that's gone. Thought can project itself into the future, but it is tied to yesterday. Thought builds its own prison and lives in it, whether it's in the future or in the past, gilded or plain. Thought can never be still; by its very nature it is restless, ever pushing and withdrawing. The machinery of thought is ever in motion, noisily or quietly, on the surface or hidden. It cannot wear itself out. Thought can refine itself, can control its wanderings, can choose its own direction and conform to environment.

Thought cannot go beyond itself; it may function in narrow or wide fields, but it will always be within the limitations of memory, and memory is always limited. Memory must die psychologically, inwardly, but function only outwardly. Inwardly there must be death and outwardly sensitivity to every challenge and response. The inward concern of thought prevents action.

September 9

To have such a beautiful day in town seems such a waste; there isn't a cloud in the sky, the sun is warm, and the pigeons are warming themselves on the roof, but the roar of the town goes on without pity. The trees feel the autumnal air, and their leaves are turning, slowly and languidly, without care. The streets are crowded with people, always looking at shops, very few at the sky. They see each other as they pass by, but they are concerned with themselves, how they look, what impression they give; envy and fear are always there in spite of their make-up, in spite of their polished appearance. The labourers are too tired, heavy, and grumbling. And the massed trees against the wall of a museum seem so utterly sufficient to themselves; the river held in by cement and stone seems so utterly indifferent. The pigeons are plentiful, with a strutting dignity of their own. And so a day passed by on the street, in the office. It's a world of monotony and despair, with laughter that soon passes away. In the evening the monuments, the streets, are lit up, but there are a vast emptiness and unbearable pain.

There's a yellow leaf on the pavement, just fallen. It's still full of summer, and though in death it's still very beautiful. Not a part of it is withered; it has still the shape and grace of spring, but it's yellow and will wither away by the evening. Early in the morning, when the sun was just showing itself in a clear sky, there was a flash of otherness, with its benediction, and the beauty of it remains. It's not that thought has captured it and holds it, but it has left its imprint on consciousness. Thought is always fragmentary, and what it holds is always partial, as memory. It cannot observe the whole; the part cannot see the whole, and the imprint of benediction is non-verbal and non-communicable through words, through any symbol. Thought will always fail in its attempt to discover, to experience that which is beyond time and space. The brain, the machinery of thought can be quiet; the very active brain can be quiet; its machinery can run very slowly. The quietness of the brain, though intensely sensitive, is essential; then only can thought disentangle itself and come to an end. The ending of thought is not death; then only can there be innocence, freshness, a new quality to thought. It's this quality that puts an end to sorrow and despair.

Saanen, 19 July 1970

YOU KNOW, FREEDOM implies the total abnegation, the denial, negation of all authority. One has to understand this very, very carefully, because the younger generation think freedom is to spit in the face of the policeman, to do whatever they want. The denial of outward authority does not necessarily mean complete freedom from all inward authority, and when we understand the inward authority and a mind and a heart that are wholly, completely, integrally free from authority, then we'll be able to understand the action of freedom outwardly. Outward freedom of action depends entirely and wholly on the mind that is free from authority inwardly. It requires a great deal of patient inquiry and deliberation to find out what it means to be free from inward authority. So if you don't mind, we will go together, share together, work together to find out what it means to be free from all inward authority.

The word *authority* according to the dictionary refers to one who has an original idea, the author of something. The original human being who has discovered something new, perhaps puts it into words, or into a picture, or a poem, or a religious life, and that becomes the pattern, the mould, a system that others follow. You have Lenin, Mao, or others—politically, economically, or religiously—then the rest follow, blindly, or cleverly, or intellectually.

Observe this in your own life, because that is what we are doing. By listening to the speaker, you are actually listening to yourself, observing yourself. Otherwise what is said has no value whatsoever.

There are patterns of life, conduct, politically or psychologically, outwardly or inwardly, and the easiest thing for the mind—which is generally very lazy, indolent—is to follow what somebody else has said. The follower then accepts authority as a means to achieve what he wants or what is promised through that particular system of philosophy or ideation. He accepts a particular system of thought, follows it, clings to it, depends on it, and thereby makes it into authority. Then he is merely a follower, a second-hand human being—and most people are completely second-hand. They may think they have some original idea about painting or writing poems, but essentially, because they are conditioned to follow, to imitate, to conform, they become second-hand, absurd human beings. That's one destructive quality of authority.

Now, do we belong in that kind of category? Do you? Find out. If we follow somebody, or some belief or instruction according to a book or a person who promises a reward—enlightenment, a thing to be achieved at the end through a particular means—the means and the giver of that means become the authority. As human beings, do we do this? Do you follow somebody psychologically? We are not talking of outward following, outward obedience, obeying a law or denying a law. We are not discussing that. Inwardly, psychologically, do you, as a human being, follow? If you do, then you are essentially a second-hand, worthless human being. You may do good works, you may have a very good life, you may have a lovely house, and so on, but it has very little meaning.

Then there is another kind of authority, the authority of tradition. The meaning of that word *tradition* is to hand over from the past to the present. There is the Christian tradition, the Catholic tradition, the family tradition, the racial tradition. Tradition also implies not only what has been handed down but also the tradition of memory, which is much more difficult. If you look at tradition, you càn see that at certain levels it has value, and at other levels it has no value at all. Good manners, politeness, consideration, thoughtfulness, the alertness of the mind that is watching, can gradually become a tradition and, the pattern having been set, the mind then just repeats it, gets up, opens the door, is punctual for meals. It is polite, but it has become a tradition; it is not born out of consideration, alertness, sharpness, and clearness.

Then there is the tradition of a mind that has cultivated memory, that functions like a computer, every action repeating over and over again, so that it can never receive anything new, it can never listen to anything totally different. Our brains are like tape recorders; certain memories have been cultivated through centuries, and we repeat that, over and over and over again. Through the noise of that repetition we try to listen to something new, and therefore we don't listen at all. Then we say, 'What am I to do? How am I to get rid of the old machinery, the old tape, and listen to the new tape?' The new thing can be heard only when the old tape is silent. And the old tape becomes completely silent without any effort if you are serious to listen, to find out, to give your attention; then there is no authority of another, and dependence on another.

There is the authority of tradition; there is the authority of the past as memory, as experience, as knowledge; and there is the authority of an immediate experience. You have an experience, and that becomes the authority. Experience is based on your past, accumulated knowledge; otherwise if you don't recognize it as experience, as something new, it is not an experience.

So there are these various categories of authority. How can a mind and heart, a brain that is so conditioned by authority, imitation, conformity, adjustment, listen to anything completely new? How can it listen to the beauty of a day when the mind and the heart and the brain are clouded by the authority of the past? Can you see—not verbally, not intellectually, but actually perceive the fact, the actual 'what is'—that a mind that is burdened by the past, conditioned by various forms of authority, is not free and therefore cannot see completely? If you actually see that, then the past is set aside without effort.

So freedom implies the complete cessation of all authority inwardly. And from that quality of mind that is free, an outward freedom comes that is entirely different from the reaction of an opposing or resisting factor. What we are saying is really quite simple, and it is because of its very simplicity that you might miss it. Our minds, our brains are conditioned through authority, through imitation and conformity. That is a fact. And therefore freedom cannot exist for such a mind. It can talk endlessly about freedom and revolt against certain outward forms of restriction, but it is not a free mind. The mind that is actually free has no inward authority whatsoever.

We have explained very carefully what authority means. Have you, as a human being, any form of authority on which you depend? If you do, you cannot have freedom, and it is only the free mind that knows what it means to love and meditate.

In understanding freedom, one has to understand also what discipline is. This may be rather contrary to all that you think, because we generally think freedom means freedom from all discipline. Let us find out together what it means. I am not laying down or telling you what you should or should not do. We are trying to find out—not trying—we are finding out what it means to discipline. What is the quality of mind that is highly disciplined? Freedom cannot exist without discipline. That doesn't mean that you must first be disciplined and then you will have freedom, but that freedom and discipline go together; they are not two separate things.

What does *discipline* mean? According to the dictionary— I'm sorry to talk about the dictionary meanings of words so much—the Latin root of that word means to learn. The disciplined mind is not the mind that conforms to a goal, not the mind that drills itself into a certain pattern of action according to an ideology or a belief of Marx, Engels, Stalin, Lenin, or Mao. It is a mind that is capable of learning, which is entirely different from a mind that is capable of conforming. A mind that conforms cannot possibly learn, but only a mind that is observing, that sees actually 'what is' and does not interpret 'what is' according to its own desires, its own conditioning, its own particular pleasure. Discipline does not mean suppression, control, conformity, or adjustment to a pattern or an ideology; it means a mind that sees 'what is' and learns from 'what is'. Such a mind has to be extraordinarily alert, aware. That is what it means to have discipline.

In the ordinary sense of the words, *to discipline oneself* implies that there is an entity that is disciplining itself according to something. That is a dualistic process. When I tell myself that I must get up early in the morning because I am lazy, or that I must not be angry, or that I should not do something, in that there is a dualistic process involved: there is the observer and the thing observed; there is the one who controls with his will what he should do or denies what he should not do. In that dualistic state there is conflict, isn't there? So discipline, as it is accepted, is a process of constant conflict. That is the discipline laid down by parents, by society, by religious organizations, by the church, by what the Buddha and Jesus and so on have said. For us discipline means conformity, and there is a revolt against conformity. Parents want you to do certain things, and you revolt against them. Our lives are based on obedience, conformity—and its opposite: denying conformity to do what one likes, revolting against the pattern. This is what is going on throughout the world.

We are going to find out what is the quality of the mind that doesn't conform, doesn't imitate, doesn't follow, doesn't obey but in itself is highly disciplined, in the sense that it is constantly learning. What is the quality of a mind that is learning, not conforming? Conformity implies comparison, doesn't it? I compare myself with another, measuring myself—what I am or what I should be—against somebody else: the hero, the saint, the Mao, the Lenin, the Marx—or if you don't like them, against Jesus. Where there is conformity, there must be comparison. Please see this and find out if you can live daily—not verbally but actually—without comparison, which means not conforming.

You know you do compare yourself, don't you? That is our conditioning from childhood—'Oh, you must be like your brother', or your great-aunt; you must be like the saint or follow what Mao or the latest says. We are always comparing; that is our education in schools: giving marks and passing examinations. You don't know what it means to live without comparison, without competition, and therefore non-aggressively, non-violently. The moment you compare yourself with another, it is a form of aggression, and therefore it is a form of violence. Violence isn't merely going and killing or hitting somebody; it is this comparative spirit: 'I must be like somebody else', or, 'I must perfect myself'. Self-improvement is the antithesis of freedom and learning. Find out for yourself how to live a life without comparing, and you will see what an extraordinary thing happens to you if you really become aware, choicelessly, of what it means to live without comparison, never using the word *better*, never using the words *I will be*. We are slaves to the words *to be*, meaning I will be somebody at some time in the future.

So comparison, conformity, go together and only breed suppression, conflict, and endless pain. Can you find a way of living—not a way—a daily living in which there is no comparison? Do it sometime, and you will see what an extraordinary thing it is. It frees you from so many burdens. And if you are aware of that, the very awareness brings about that quality of mind that is highly sensitive and therefore highly disciplined, because it is constantly learning—not what it wants to learn, or what is pleasurable to learn, what is gratifying to learn, but *learning*.

Can you become aware of authority and of following it, of obedience and conformity to a pattern, to tradition, to propaganda, to what other people have said? The tradition, the accumulated experiences of yourself or of others, of the race or of the family, all become the authority. And where there is authority, the mind can never be free to discover whatever there is to be discovered, something entirely timelessly new. A mind that is sensitive has no pattern. It is constantly moving; it is like a river, flowing, and in that flow there is no suppression, no conformity, no desire to fulfil and all that rubbish. It is only the mind that is static that says, 'I must fulfil', 'I must become'.

We must clearly, deeply, and seriously understand the nature of a mind that is free and therefore truly religious, free from all dependence inwardly. Because dependence on something, on a person—on a friend, or on a husband, wife—or on some idea, authority, breeds fear. It is very important to understand, before we go into all the complicated things of life, that a mind must be completely free from all authority inwardly, because that is the source of fear. If I depend on you for my comfort, if I depend upon you because you applaud me when I speak, if I depend on you as an escape from my own loneliness, ugliness, stupidity, my own shallowness, pettiness, shoddiness, then depending on you breeds fear. Depending on any form of subjective imagination, fantasy, experience, knowledge, does destroy freedom.

Now, after saying all that, I want to find out—don't you?—if one does depend. Because a mind that depends on something is not alone, clean, healthy, sane. If your mind depends on Mao, Lenin, and all those people on the one hand, what kind of mind is it? You have only thrown away the old and taken on the new, but the quality of the mind is the same. And on the opposite hand, unfortunately, are all the religious leaders, from the infinite past to the present; and if you depend on them, look what you are doing to yourself. You are depending on somebody else's authority about what they think is true. And what they think is the truth is not the truth. So you are lost; you are confused. Out of that confusion we do a great many things; we join this or that, we become activists or meditate, run away to Japan to sit in some Zen school, or to India.

When you are aware of all this—please do be—when you are aware of the left, the right, and the centre, you are learning. You see that it all implies a dependence inwardly, and therefore there is no freedom; therefore there is fear. It is only a confused mind that depends, not a clear mind. Being confused, you say, 'I must depend', and then you say, 'How am I to be free from dependence?'—which becomes another conflict. But if you observe the truth very clearly that if a mind depends inwardly on any authority—whether the authority is a word, a symbol, an ideology, a person—that dependency creates confusion, then you will cease to depend. So your mind becomes extraordinarily sensitive and therefore capable of learning. It is like a child who learns. He is very curious; he wants to find out. That very sensitivity is the quality of a mind that is constantly learning and so disciplining itself without any form of compulsion, conformity.

Is this all somewhat clear, not verbally but actually? I can imagine or think I am very clear, but that clarity may be very short-lived. The quality of clear perception comes only when there is no dependence and therefore no confusion. Confusion arises only when there is fear. Can you honestly, seriously, find out whether you are free from authority? That needs tremendous inquiry into yourself, great awareness, doesn't it? And from that clarity there is a totally different kind of action that is not fragmentary, that is not divided politically, religiously. It is a total action.

Would you like to discuss what we have talked about?

Questioner: From what you said, it seems that the same action can at one point be thought a reaction to some kind of an outward authority, and at another point or at the same time by another individual, it can be a total action.

Krishnamurti: Quite right, sir. Look, sir, we can spin along intellectually and verbally beat each other or explain things to each other, but that doesn't mean a thing. What to you may be a complete action may appear to me as incomplete action. That is not the point. The point is whether or not your mind, as a human being, is alive. A human being is the world—he is not an individual. *Individual* means indivisible. An individual is one who is undivided in himself, who is non-fragmentary, not broken up; he is whole. *Whole* means sane, healthy, and *whole* also means holy, h-o-l-y. You are not that; when you talk about, 'I am an individual', you are nothing of the kind.

So live a life, sir, of no authority, of no comparison. Do it, and you will find out what an extraordinary thing it is. You are alive; you have tremendous energy when you are not competing, not comparing. You are not suppressing, you are living, and therefore you are sane, whole, and therefore sacred.

Q: Do you think it is possible to learn all the time?

K: I want to learn; is it possible to learn all the time? Now when you ask that question you have already made it difficult for yourself. Right? 'Can I learn all the time? It is impossible.' You see, by putting a question of that kind, you are preventing yourself from learning. Look, sir, I am not concerned whether I am going to learn all the time. I'll find out. What I am concerned with is: Am I learning? If I am learning, I am not concerned with whether or not it is all the time; I don't make a problem of it. When you say, 'My God, how am I to give my whole attention all the time?' it is impossible. But if you say, 'Look, I am learning', you are not concerned with whether you are going to learn all day and all night; you are learning. A mind that is learning never puts that question. Then that question becomes irrelevant. If I am learning, I am learning all the time.

Q: You can learn from anything.

K: You can learn from anything—that is, if you are aware, you are learning. Look, sir, this is very complex; may I go into it a little bit?

Can I learn all the time? Which is important here, learning or all the time? Learning. Now, when I am learning, I am not concerned with time, the time interval, time period. I am only concerned with what I am learning, that I am learning. Now, mind goes off, naturally; it gets tired, then it becomes inattentive. Being inattentive, it does all kinds of stupid things. So it is not a question of how to make the mind that is inattentive become attentive. What is important is for the inattentive mind to become aware that it is inattentive.

Look, say I am aware, watching everything, watching the movement of the tree, the water, the flow of a mountain, watching myself, watching, not correcting, not saying this should be or this should not be, just watching. Naturally the mind that is watching gets tired. When it gets tired, it is inattentive. Being inattentive, it suddenly becomes aware that it is inattentive; therefore it tries to force itself to become attentive. Right? So there is a conflict between inattention and attention. I say, don't do that but become aware that you are inattentive. That's all.

Q: Could you describe when you are aware that you are inattentive?

K: No, no, no. I am *learning*. Look, I am learning about myself. Right? I am not learning according to some psychologist or specialist. I am learning, I am watching, and I see something in myself. I don't condemn it, I don't judge it, I don't push it aside, I just watch it. I watch that I am proud—let's take that as an example. I don't say, 'I must put it aside, how ugly to be proud'. I just watch it. As I am watching, I am learning. Watching means learning what pride involves, how it has come into being, how stupid it is. I watch it. I can't watch it more than, say, five or six minutes— if you can, that is a great deal—the next moment it becomes inattentive. Now having been attentive and then knowing what inattention is, you struggle to make inattention attentive. Don't you do all these things? I said, don't do that but watch inattention, become aware that you are inattentive. That's all. Stop there. Don't say you must spend all your time being attentive but just watch when you are inattentive. Full stop.

I don't want to go any further into this because it is really quite complex. Because there is a quality of mind that is all the time awake, all the time watching, and therefore, merely watching, there is nothing to learn. And that means a mind that is extraordinarily quiet, extraordinarily silent. What has a silent clear mind to learn? I won't go into all that.

Brockwood Park,
12 September 1970

I SEE—THE mind observes—that a mind that is very clear has no choice, has no need of choice, and therefore the whole response of action according to will completely comes to an end. Will implies resistance. Obviously. And any form of resistance is isolation. A mind that is isolated is not a free mind, and a mind that is caught up in the acquisition of knowledge as a means to freedom doesn't come up with that freedom; it doesn't happen to it. So one has to go into the question of knowledge.

Why has knowledge become such an extraordinarily important thing in life? Knowledge is accumulated experience, both outward experience that thousands of people have discovered—scientifically, psychologically, and so on—and also the knowledge one has acquired for oneself through observation, through learning, through searching. What place has knowledge in freedom? Does this interest you?

Audience: Yes.

Krishnamurti: No, no, don't be so quick in answering yes, because this is not a verbal exchange, an intellectual play. Knowledge is always in the past. When you say, 'I know', it implies you have known. Knowledge of every kind—scientific, personal, communal, or whatever it is—is always in the past. Can a mind that lives in the past, is the result of the past, be free at all? Knowledge is not only about facts and information and so on; knowledge includes the image, the symbol, the image that I have built about you and that you have built about me.

Questioner: What about self-knowledge?

K: First see how the mind accumulates knowledge, why it accumulates, where it is necessary, and where it becomes an impediment to freedom. To do anything one must have knowledge: driving a car, speaking a language, doing a technological job, you must have abundance of knowledge—the more efficient, the more objective, the more impersonal, the better. Knowledge is necessary. But can a mind that is full of information as knowledge ever be free, or must it always carry that knowledge, which is always the past? From carrying that past, that knowledge, and meeting the present with that comes conflict. I met you yesterday, and you flattered me or insulted me so I have that image of you; that is part of knowledge. With that knowledge, with that image I have built about you, which is the past, I meet you today. And therefore there is conflict between you and me. This is simple enough.

So the observer is the reservoir of knowledge. Please discover this yourself; it's more fun. Therefore the observer is the past; he is the censor, the entity that has accumulated knowledge, and from that knowledge he judges, he evaluates. And he is doing exactly the same with regard to himself. He has acquired knowledge about himself through psychologists; he has learned what he is, or he thinks he has learned about himself, and with that knowledge he looks at himself. He doesn't look at himself with fresh eyes. He says, 'I know; I have seen myself. It's rather ugly; parts of it are extraordinarily nice, but the other parts are rather terrible'. He has already judged, and his judgment is based on the past, which is his knowledge about himself. Therefore he never discovers anything new about himself, because the observer is different from the thing observed, which he calls himself.

And that's what we are doing all the time in all relationships, in mechanical relationships or human relationships, relationship with the machine, or relationship with another. It is all based on the desire to find a place where we can be completely secure, certain, and we have sought and found security in knowledge. The keeper of this knowledge is the observer, the censor, the thinker, the experiencer; and the observer is always watching as being different from the thing observed. The observer analyses himself, or he is analysed by the professional—who himself needs analysing—and playing this game goes on.

So one asks if one can look at this whole movement of life without the burden of the past. That's what we are all trying to do, aren't we? We want to find new expressions. If you are an artist, you want to be more objective—you know, you play with that game forever and ever—you want to write new books, a new way of looking at life, a new way of living. You want to revolt against the old and fall into the trap of the new, which is the reaction to the old.

One sees that intelligence doesn't lie in the hands of the observer; it is only when the mind is free, free to learn—and learning is not the accumulation of knowledge. On the contrary, learning is movement, and accumulation of knowledge is static. You may add to it, but the core of it is static, and from this static state one functions, one lives, one paints, one writes, one does all the mischief in the world. And you call that freedom. So can the mind be free of the known?

You know it is really quite an extraordinary question if you ask—not merely intellectually but really very, very deeply— to find out whether the mind can ever be free from the known. Otherwise there is no creation; otherwise there is nothing new. There is nothing new under the sun then; it is always reformation of the reformed.

One has to find out why this division between the observer and the observed exists and whether there is the possibility of a mind going beyond this division. That means the possibility of being free from the known to function at a different dimension altogether, which is intelligence that will use knowledge only when necessary. So intelligence implies freedom—but not to do what one wants, which is so immature and childish. Freedom implies the cessation of all conflict; and that comes to an end only when the observer is the observed, because then there is no division.

After all, freedom exists when there is love, doesn't it? You know, that word is so terribly loaded, like *God*. One hesitates to use the word *love* because it is associated with pleasure, with sex, with fear, with jealousy, with dependency, with acquisitiveness, and all the rest of it. A mind that is not free does not know what love means. It may know pleasure and hence know what fear is. But fear and desire and pleasure are certainly not love; that can only come into being when there is real freedom from the past. Is that ever possible? You know man has sought in different ways to be free from the transiency of knowledge, and so he has always sought something beyond knowledge, beyond thought. Thought is the response of knowledge. So he has created an image called God and all the absurdities that arise around that. But to find out if there is something that is beyond the image of thought, there must be freedom from all fear.

Q: Could I ask if you are differentiating between the cells of the brain as intellect and the mind that is an awareness beyond the actual intellect?

K: No, I think we are not dividing it. We are using mind as the total process of thought, as memory, as knowledge, including the brain cells. Obviously. One can't separate the brain cells from the rest of the mind, can one?

Q: The brain builds up intellect.

K: What is the function of the brain? What is the brain? We are not talking professionally—I don't read books about all this business—but what is the brain?

Q: Well, it is a computer.

K: A most extraordinary computer, built, put together for thousands of years. It is the result of time. Time is memory. Memory is experience, accumulation of thousands of years of experience to survive, to be secure, to be safe. Therefore one has this knowledge, especially about the outer, knowledge of everything that is happening in the outer world, how to go to the moon—but very little about oneself.

Q: Could creation depend on memory and therefore depend on the past?

K: Does it? Now, wait a minute, sir. Creation depends on memory?

Q: What I was suggesting in fact was what you said earlier that there is nothing new under the sun.

K: That's what we think, sir, that there is nothing new under the sun. At least the Bible says so; Ecclesiastes says so. Now, aren't we confusing creation with expression? Does a creative person need expression? I need expression to fulfil myself—I must express; I have a feeling that I am an artist, and I must put it down in paint or in a poem. Does creation need expression at all? And does expression indicate a mind that is free in creation? Because one writes a poem, or paints a picture, does that indicate a creative mind?

Q: Not necessarily.

K: Therefore what does creativeness mean? Not the mechanical repetition of the past.

Q: I think creativeness does need expression.

K: Wait, we will go slowly. Does creativeness need expression? I am just asking. You say it does need it. Then it is finished; there is no further inquiry. We are just learning. We are learning together. Please, do bear in mind all the time that we are learning together, that we are working together, sharing together, and therefore if you say it needs it, then it is finished, the door is shut in my face.

Let's go into it slowly. What does creativeness mean? What is the feeling of the mind that feels creative? Do you know it?

Q: When the mind is inspired, then it creates something new.

K: When the mind sees something good and beautiful, that's a creative mind? Does a creative mind need inspiration? No, sir, you see you make statements. Do inquire. Let's proceed slowly into it. I don't know what it means. We are going to find out, not verbally but, you know, actually find out what a mind that is really extraordinarily creative means.

Q: It means reality.

K: You say it is reality. Is your mind creative to know that it is reality? Look, sir, please, mustn't the mind be free to be creative—free? Otherwise it is repetitive; in that repetitiveness there may be new expressions, but it is still repetitive, mechanical. Can a mind, a life, that is mechanical be creative? Can a mind, a human being that is in conflict, in tension, neurotic, be creative? He may write marvellous poems, marvellous plays—he might write a marvellous play after having a hang-over or be 'hooked on' something. Those are all the new phrases.

Q: You must be in the 'now'.

K: Therefore sir, what does that mean, to be in the now? It cannot be mechanical. It cannot be burdened with all the weight of knowledge, as tradition. It means a mind that is really profoundly free of fear. That's freedom, isn't it?

Q: Surely it must seek safety still; that's a function of the brain.

K: Look, sir, you are saying there must be security.

Q: It is the function of the brain.

K: Of course, it is the function of the brain to be secure. It can function properly, efficiently, clearly, when it is secure. But is it secure when it divides itself into nationalities, into religions, into saying, 'It's mine; it's yours'? Where there is any form of division, there is destruction—the Jews, the Moslems, the Arabs.

Q: It seems to me that without opposition there is no growth.

K: Oh, without opposition there is no growth. Oh, my lord! That's part of our conditioning, isn't it?

Q: No, it's part of reality.

K: Is it, is it? Let's find out, madam.

Q: Without a high there is no low.

K: Let's find out. We have lived that way, between the good and the bad, between hate and love, in jealousy, between tenderness and brutality, between violence and gentleness. That's how we have lived for millions of years, and we have accepted that because we are conditioned that it is something real. Is it—to live like this?

Q: How can one be free of this conditioning?

K: Now, we are discussing what is the mind, what is the quality of the mind that is creative. Can a quality of mind that wavers between hate and jealousy and love and pleasure and fear know what love means? Can a mind that is always seeking expression, fulfilment, to become famous, to be recognized, to be somebody? We all call that fulfilment, becoming, being, you know, all the rest of it, which is all part of the social structure, part of our conditioning. Can such a mind be creative when it is caught in the word, or the verb *to be?* To be: 'I have been; I will be'—always becoming something—can such a mind be creative? In becoming there is fear: you might not become; you might not be successful. In becoming there is the fear of death, fear of the unknown, so you cling to the known, which is knowledge. Can such a mind ever be creative? Or is creation the result of stress, opposition, strain?

Q: Creativeness is joy and attention, imagination.

K: Oh, creativeness is joy, imagination. You see we are all so—I don't know what we are. Do you know what joy means? Is joy pleasure?

Q: No.

K: You say no, but that's what you are seeking, aren't you? You have a moment of great ecstasy, great joy, and you think about it. The thinking about it has reduced it to pleasure. So sir, please, we are all so full of conclusions, and a mind that has a number of conclusions is not a free mind. Find out whether one can live without any conclusion, live daily without any conclusion. That means to live a life without comparison. You conclude because you compare. To live a life without comparison!—you do it some time, and you will find out what an extraordinary thing takes place.

Q: If I'm just the experience, and the experience is fear or anger, what happens?

K: If one is only experience, the questioner asks, and the experiencer is fear, but only lives in experience without that experience being recorded and recognized in the future as an experience, what happens? Is that it? I think one has first to find out what we mean by that word *experience*. Doesn't it mean to go through? Doesn't it imply recognition? Otherwise you wouldn't know you had experience. Are we meeting each other? If I didn't recognize the experience, would it be experience?

Q: Can't there be just experience without the image?

K: Wouldn't you go a little further and ask why you need experience at all? We all want experience. First we are bored with our life; we have made life into a mechanical affair, and we are bored with it. We want wider, deeper experiences, transcendental experiences. Right? Now what does all this imply? Boredom, and the escapes from this boredom, through meditation, through various ways into the so-called *divine*—whatever that is—which are all formulas. Experience implies a recognition, and you can only recognize if there is a memory of that thing that you have already experienced; otherwise there is no recognition. So the question is, why do we ask for experience at all? To wake us up because we are asleep? A new challenge is an experience, but we respond to that challenge according to our background, which is the known. So there is always conflict between the challenge and the response.

So is it possible to live a life in which the mind is so clear, awake, so much a light to itself, that it needs no experience? Don't say yes; find out! That means to live a life without conflict. That means a mind that is highly sensitive and therefore intelligent, which is a light in itself, and therefore it doesn't need something to challenge it or to awaken it. Right?

Saanen, 15 July 1973

ONE REALIZES IN all seriousness that what the world is we are, and we are the world. How is the human mind to change—the mind that has been cultivated through millennia, the mind that has been educated, conditioned, shaped by the environment in which it lives, by the culture in which it has flowered? This mind has taken time, ten thousand years or more, to arrive at what we are now. That mind is full of experiences, knowledge, images, symbols. We are asking what place knowledge has in the transformation of the human mind. We have acquired a great deal of knowledge, technologically, in so many ways, in so many departments, in science, biology, anthropology, medicine, and so on and so on. We have also acquired a great deal of knowledge in the field, the area, of the psyche. Knowledge being the past, what is its relationship to the transformation of the human mind?

I have a great deal of knowledge about myself: why I think certain things, what the associations of a particular thought are, why I react, my experiences, my hurts, my anxieties, my fears, my insistent pursuit of pleasure, and the fears of living and dying. I have accumulated tremendous knowledge about myself. I have watched very carefully for fifty years, carefully observed all the subtleties, the cunning, the deceptions, the cruelties. I have watched; I have listened to dozens of philosophers, teachers, gurus. They gave their knowledge, their experience. When I am talking about myself, I am talking about you; don't put the cap on me and look at me and forget yourself. We are talking about you.

So during these years—whether it is ten years, or fifty years, or a hundred years, or ten thousand years—a great deal of knowledge has been accumulated. And yet I am just a mediocre, shoddy, second-hand, cunning, stupid human being. I react so quickly to violence, to flattery; my vanities and pride are immense. I conform; I battle against conformity. I talk about art, teach a little bit of art here and there, play an instrument, write a little book, become famous, notorious, wanting publicity—you know—I am all that. I have gathered tremendous information, knowledge, and that knowledge is the past. All knowledge is the past. There is no future knowledge; there is no present knowledge. There is only knowledge as the past. And knowledge is time.

Now I say to myself, 'I know this'. And also, by careful objective, non-personal observation of the world, I see there must be total change in me as a human being. I see that in my relationship with another, with my neighbour, with human beings—whether intimate or with a man ten thousand miles away—there is a battle, conflict, misery. I see that I am always asserting myself, the selfish activity, the self-centred movement. And that is all knowledge.

Now what place has knowledge in human transformation, which the mind sees is absolutely necessary? That is the question. Will future experience, taking time, gathering more and more knowledge—not only to go to the moon and in various other fields but also knowledge about myself—bring about change? That is, will time and knowledge—and knowledge is time—bring transformation in me, in you? Or is quite a different kind of energy demanded?

Are we meeting each other? We are sharing the thing together, and to share something together, we both need a relationship of affection, consideration, inquiry; otherwise we can't share. We must both be interested in the thing we are sharing together; that means sharing together at the same time, at the same level, with the same intensity.

So I have this problem; you have this problem. We know a great deal of what others have said about us, and we know about ourselves. Will that bring about change? That means, will thought change the human mind? Thought is the response of knowledge. Thought has created this world. Thought has divided people as Christians and non-Christians, as the Arab and the Jew, as the Catholic and the non-Catholic, the communist and the Hindu. Thought has divided people. Are you aware of it? Thought has divided the world as Switzerland, France, Germany, Russia, and so on. Thought has brought about conflict between one another, not only religiously, socially, economically, but also in our relationships. And we are looking to thought to change us. That is what we are doing, aren't we? We may not be conscious of it, but actually that is what we are trying to do.

Is the picture clear—not *my* picture but *the* picture—that thought/knowledge/time, which are all the same, has brought about this world with all its confusion, misery, corruption, sorrow, pain—out there and also in here? And we say it all must change. Serious people say that—but they employ thought to bring about a change.

So I question the whole thing. I see very clearly that knowledge cannot change my activity, my self-centred movement of 'you' and 'me' as two separate entities fighting each other. So what am I to do? Do put this question to yourself in all seriousness. What is your answer? You see the world, and see yourself as the world, and you see what knowledge is, knowing knowledge is necessary in certain fields of activity, and also asking yourself if that knowledge—which human beings have gathered for thousands of years—can bring about a radical psychological revolution. Now take that thought; look at it. How do you listen to that statement? How do you listen to the statement: what place has knowledge in human transformation? When you listen to those words, do you translate them into an abstraction? From listening to that statement, do you draw a conclusion that is an abstraction, and therefore you are not listening to the statement but listening to the abstraction?

I have asked a question: what place has time, which is knowledge and thought, in the transformation of the mind of a human being? Because there must be transformation. Now how do you listen to it? Do you listen merely to the meaning of words? Or do you, in the very act of listening, draw a conclusion, and therefore you are listening with a conclusion and not actually listening to the question? You see the difference? When you listen to the statement and draw a conclusion, make an abstraction, then thought is in action. I am not being clever; this is not an intellectual thing. You can observe it in yourself.

Can you think without a word, without an image, without a symbol? I am asking you that question. Can you think without a word, without a symbol, without an image? If there is no image, no symbol, no word, is there thinking? Now you listen to that—what do you do with the act of listening? What have you done after listening to it? Go on, please. You are trying to find out, aren't you, if there is a thinking without a word. And you say, 'By Jove, I can't think without a word. I must have an image, a symbol; otherwise there is no thinking'. So the thinking, the word, the symbol, the image are knowledge. And that is time. So can that time change the human mind? All philosophies, all religious structures, are based on thinking, which is knowledge, and we are looking to that knowledge to bring about a change. I say that is not possible. But I must see that very clearly, see it in the sense of being sensitive to the truth of that statement. The truth is that knowledge, although it is necessary in the world of action—driving a car, learning a language, scientific study, and so on—it has no place whatsoever in the transforming of a human being.

Do you see the truth of it? You can only see the truth of it if you don't draw a conclusion from it. You will say, 'Then what am I to do?' That is a conclusion. 'Then how shall I act? I have lived all my life in conclusions, beliefs, ideas, thought, and you come along and say, "Look, that has no place in relationship, in human change".' Then you ask, 'What will take its place?' That question is put by thought, so you are still functioning in the field of thought, and therefore you don't see the truth of it.

You see, the chief concern for a serious man is the total transformation of the human mind—total, not partial, complete revolution in the psyche—because that is the first movement that can transform the outward environment. Without that radical change, mere outward change has no meaning because it creates more and more and more problems. You can see how people are polluting the earth, the waters, and mere reformation is not going to change that. So being serious, one asks: if knowledge has no place, then what is the energy, what is the flame, what is the quality that will completely change the mind? Now, do I, do you, see clearly the truth that knowledge is not going to change man? Not because I say it, not because I am convincing you intellectually, and not because you feel that is the only way, but do you, irrespective of your environment, irrespective of the speaker, irrespective of any influence, impressions, demands, see the truth of it for yourself? If you do, then what is the state of your mind? What is the state of the mind that sees the truth or falseness of a statement? What is your mind that says, 'Yes, that is true'? Can you answer? Is it an intellectual conviction and therefore not truth? Is it an opinion sustained by reason and therefore not true? Is it a logical sequence, which you accept and therefore not true? Or is it a dialectical opinion, which is seeing the truth through opinions and therefore not truth?

What is the quality of a mind facing this statement? How does it receive it? Is it capable of looking at that statement as though hearing it for the first time and seeing instantly the fact of it?

We will leave it there for the moment.

Perhaps you would like to ask some questions relevant to the things we have been talking about.

Questioner: I don't see why knowledge is time.

Krishnamurti: Don't you see it really? Look, I don't know how to ride a bicycle, so it will take time to learn it. I don't know how to speak Russian; it will take time to learn it. To learn the language with all its knowledge will take time, time to cover it from here to there. And I require knowledge to go from here to there. So obviously, there is no question about this, all knowledge is time. And all knowledge is the past.

Q: You don't need time at all; you can use knowledge now.

K: Having accumulated knowledge as time, you can use it in the present. Is that it? Now listen to that: having accumulated knowledge, having learned English, I use that knowledge, that language, in the present. That is obvious; I am doing it. In my relationship with you I have built knowledge about you, and that has taken time, and I use that knowledge in my relationship with you in the present. So I use the past to look at you in my relationship. I use the image that I have about you in my relationship; the image functions. So that image, which is the past, divides you and me.

Q: What if you are looking at an individual who is in himself the result of the past? To see him, mustn't you look also at the past because he is it?

K: Of course. To look at myself, which is the past, do I use the eyes of the past to look at myself? If I do use the eyes of the past to look at myself, there is no looking at myself.

Q: They are my only eyes.

K: Wait. I do not look at myself. I can only look at myself with eyes that are not of the past. All this is obvious.

Q: How can I change my mind instantly?

K: You have put the wrong question, sir. You know, to answer that question, one has to go into the whole question of time. And that is an immense question, not for the moment. Can the mind change instantly? That is, can the mind—which is of time, put together by time, put together by knowledge, put together by experience—can that whole mind—the mind being the heart, the whole works—change radically outside of time? Not instantly. I say, in all humility, that it can; otherwise I wouldn't be talking about it. I would be a hypocrite if I talked about it then. I would be indulging in ideas, which is stupid.

You know, this whole problem of the place of knowledge is extraordinarily intricate, subtle, because, you see, on one side you *need* to have knowledge. I have to have knowledge to go to where I live, to drive a car, to speak this language, to recognize you, to play golf, tennis, to go to the factory. To do anything, I must have knowledge. And yet I see knowledge has no place—or has it a place?—in human change. This requires enormous, wide, and swift perception—not a conclusion. I can conclude and say, 'Well it has a place', or, 'It has no place'—that has no meaning. But to see the whole field of knowledge, and to see where knowledge is necessary and where it becomes a destructive thing, requires great intelligence.

So is intelligence the product of time? Do listen to it. Don't agree or disagree. Is intelligence personal, yours or mine? Or is intelligence the seeing of this whole movement of knowledge? To see it, you must be highly sensitive, be attentive; you must have care, affection, love. Otherwise you can't see the beauty, the swiftness of intelligence.

Brockwood Park, 6 September 1973

Krishnamurti: Putting all our questions together, I wonder what is the central issue in all this. I would say, subject to your correction, that we have many problems, imposed by society or the culture in which we live, or our own individual personal problems. And we want to resolve them all: the observer and the observed, the conscious and the unconscious, the interference of thought in seeing and acting. We have all these many problems: ill health, yoga, standing on your head, the meaning of responsibility, what love is, what happens when we die, and so on. Now who is going to answer all these questions? These are all our problems, collective, personal, quite impersonal, objective, and so on. Now who is going to answer all these questions? Suppose there were nobody of whom you could ask these questions? How would you resolve these questions and the problems that arise? That is the central issue in all this, isn't it?

Questioner: Be aware.

K: No, please, let us explore it. Don't say, 'Be aware'; that stops it, please.

First of all, we are accustomed to ask questions and to have somebody give the answers. The world is in such a frightful mess. The dictator says, 'We have the answer'. The politician says,

'We have the answer', or the economist, the socialist, or the religious person. Now you don't look to any of these people because they have all led us up the garden path, because they are responsible, as well as we are, for the misery, confusion, sorrow, starvation, wars, and violence. If we don't look to any of these people, how will we find out? There is no authority—right?—no book, no leader, no guru. How will you answer these questions? I hope you are in that position, that you are not following anybody, that there is no authority who will say, 'Do this', or, 'Don't do that'. How will you set about answering these many questions and many problems that arise in our daily life?

Q: Sir, I ask myself, and I still find I have no answers. I don't expect there are any though, are there?

K: Madam, just wait a minute. Are you in the position where you say, 'I have nobody on whom I can depend for the right answer, no book, no system, and I am left naked, and I have to find the answer, because my life is very short and I want to live a life that is completely full, rich, beautiful, intelligent, *intelligent,* and nobody can tell me what to do'? Are we in that position? No?

Q: Yes.

K: Don't say yes or no. It is one of the most difficult things to be in that position, isn't it?

So not relying on anybody, how shall I find the answer, or resolve the problems that arise every day? There isn't one series, one set of problems; problems are always arising. How shall I meet them, resolve them, not be caught in the trap of all this? Where shall I start? Surely that is the only way to find out what is truth, what is a state of mind that has no problem, that is not in conflict, that is supremely sensitive, intelligent, and so on. Now where shall I start?

Q: By looking.

K: Looking at what?

Q: Looking at the problem.

K: Looking at the problem? Who is the creator of these problems? Where shall I look for an answer?

Q: Faith.

Questioner 2: In all that is good and true.

K: Oh, no, madam, don't say all that is good and true and noble, please. Look, I am asking you a very serious question, and you say, 'Look for all that is noble and true and beautiful'. Keats, all the poets, the philosophers and all the writers and intellectuals talked about it endlessly, but that doesn't answer my question.

Q: By seeing everything that the problem is not.

K: Look, sir, I personally don't read any philosophy, psychology, don't follow any guru, any authority. To me, authority is poison, either politically or religiously. And I don't read all the sacred books in India, or here, or in Japan, or in China. They bore me. Now where shall I start? I have no confidence in myself either—right? Because I am what the world has made me, so I can't rely on myself. I don't know if you follow all this. So I say to myself, I must understand myself; myself is the world, and the world is me. And I mean that; it is not just words. And in understanding myself, I understand the world. The world about me—nature, the structure of human relationship, the divisions, the quarrels, the antagonisms, the wars, the violence, and so on—is all buried in me, because I am the world. So I must start with myself.

Q: If you are the world and the world is you, how can you start with yourself?

K: I start with what I have, sir. Shall I go on? Do please move. It is a hot morning, rather lovely. Let's get going.

I know nothing about myself. I don't start with a conclusion that I am God or I am not God, I am the State or I am not the State, that I am the world or I am not the world. I know nothing. Right? So I begin there. I know nothing. What I know is what other people have told me. Propaganda. What I know, what I am, is the result of what others have made me, or I act in reaction to the world. So I really don't know anything. So I can begin to learn.

May I go on? Please, share together.

As I know nothing, I begin to learn. So I must find out what it means to learn. What does it mean to learn? Not knowing anything, what does it mean to learn? I know I have to learn a language—Italian, Greek, French, or whatever it is. And I store up the words, the meanings of the words, the verbs, the irregular verbs, and so on. So I know a language. I know how to ride a bicycle, drive a car, dig in the garden, or run a machine. I know all that. But actually, beyond technological knowledge, I know absolutely nothing about myself. Can we start from there? Can you honestly say, 'I really don't know anything about myself'?—not out of despair, not out of a sense of frustration so that, not knowing myself, I am going to commit suicide!

Q: What do you mean by saying you know nothing about yourself?

K: What I am. Why I do this. Why I think that. What are the motives, the impressions. I know nothing about myself except the technological knowledge, the information, the activity in that field. So I know nothing about myself; I only know what people have said to me about myself. I have put aside the philosophers, the analysts, the psychoanalysts, the mothers, the fathers, the books. So I am going to learn—learn about myself—and so before I use that word, I must find out what it means to learn.

I have learned how to ride a bicycle; I have learned how to drive a car, speak a language, run a machine, or whatever it is. If I am a bureaucrat, I have learned how to push a pencil around. I know all that, but what does it mean to learn?

Q: I must be curious.

K: Curiosity. I know what that word means, but will curiosity teach me what it means to learn? I want to learn about myself. What does it mean to learn? If I learn about myself, does that learning lead to knowledge about myself, and from that knowledge I act? I want to learn about myself. Learn—what does that mean? I have learned a language, to ride a bicycle, and so on, but myself is a living thing, isn't it?—changing, demanding, asking, with lust, anger, all that. I must learn about all that. Now, if I learn about anger, that learning can leave a residue as knowledge. From that knowledge I act. Therefore I have stopped learning.

Q: One mustn't accumulate.

K: Sir, if the mind accumulates knowledge about itself, the next action or next learning is from that knowledge.

Q: I said I must not accumulate.

K: That is just it. So learning is a process of not accumulating knowledge. I have accumulated knowledge—how to ride a bicycle, speak a language, all that—but when I am learning about myself, any form of accumulation as knowledge about myself will prevent further learning. Because the 'me' is a living thing; it is not a dead thing. Therefore the mind must come to it each day, each minute afresh; otherwise it can't learn.

In learning about myself, if there is any form of accumulation in that learning, as knowledge, as experience, then further learning is impeded by the past. Therefore is it possible to learn without accumulation? That is very important for me to find out. Because if I am learning and accumulation goes on, there is no learning. Because the 'me' is a terribly living thing, very active. So the mind must be as swift, as sensitive, as subtle as the living thing. Is my mind capable of that? Please follow this step by step, and you will come to it yourself.

Q: Sir, when you look at something, as soon as you begin to think about it, life has gone on.

K: No, sir. Look, you are saying life goes on so rapidly, so quickly, so subtly, that learning is not possible. Is that it?

Q: No, I didn't say that. I said that the difficulty is that as soon as one thinks about something, one has to be able to see it and immediately pass on without trying to think about it or grasp it in any way.

K: The incident or the happening takes place so rapidly that thinking about it is no good. Therefore I must learn to observe without the previous knowledge that I have accumulated—right? That is the act of learning.

Q: Therefore one carefully watches one's motives in action.

K: No, sir. We haven't come to that. I want to know about myself. I have to learn about myself. What does learning mean? Until I find that out, I am merely accumulating knowledge about myself. And you have knowledge about yourself, haven't you?—what the psychologists have said, what the philosophers have said, what the religious books have said, what the speaker has said. So you have knowledge of all that, and when you brush aside all that, you are left with nothing; therefore you have to learn. So I am inquiring into what it means to learn.

Q: Would learning be a spontaneous realization, without reaction?

K: Spontaneous realization—I don't know what those words mean, I am sorry. We are not spontaneous, are we? We are so conditioned, so heavily burdened with the past, with all the knowledge, information, how can the mind be spontaneous?

Q: Is not the word *learning* associated with accumulation?

K: Therefore, sir, knowing that learning is associated with accumulation of knowledge, we are trying to separate them. We can't use other words. So I am learning about myself; therefore I am not accumulating knowledge about myself. If I do, then that knowledge will prevent further learning about myself. It is fairly simple, sir, isn't it?

Q: To learn, you have to have observation.

K: So how do I learn and observe, observe myself and in the act of observation learn? Now what does observation mean? Can I watch myself, all the movements of myself, without any distortion, without any previous conclusion that will bring about the distortion that I am good, that I am bad, that I am divine, that I am marvellous, that I am the most beautiful, lovely person, and so on, and so on? Can I observe myself without any shadow of distortion?

Q: If I don't try to change myself.

K: Sir, please do hold it. Look at it, sir. Can you look at yourself without any opinion about yourself?

Q: Learning is something that has to be practised, like a baby, a child learning to walk.

K: Now, do start *now!* Let's not talk about a baby, but do start learning now. Please listen to this. Can the mind observe its activity without prejudice? Prejudice is a judgment, an evaluation that has already been made, and through those eyes I look at myself. Can I observe the movement of myself in daily life—cooking, washing, all that—*and* the activity of the mind, observe without any conclusion, prejudice? You say that is not possible. Wait. Do it! Please, do these things.

Q: How do you do it?

K: I am showing it to you. Not how; I am showing it to you. Watch your mind without prejudice. Can you watch it?

Q: Please excuse me. I find as I walk about here doing this and that, there is a movement, a momentum of making judgments, prejudicing. I can feel its quality almost. Can I observe all that without judging?

K: That is what I am asking you, sir. Can the mind watch its activity without any prejudice, conclusion, judgment, evaluation, the past? Can it watch? Until it does, it is not capable of learning.

Q: Do you mean observation without thought?

K: Right. Observation without thought. I didn't want to put it that way because then you will go off into 'How am I to prevent thought from interfering?'

Q: Isn't that what you have to consider? How am I to look at thought interfering without prejudice, without judging it?

K: Now, there is nobody to answer that question. What will you do?

Q: Squirm.

K: Squirm? Then squirm! But you have to answer that question. It is no good merely squirming; you have to answer it. Life challenges you. You can't say, 'Well, I'll squirm', and leave it at that. Life says, answer it. You are a grown-up man!

Please, just a minute, sir. You see, it becomes really quite impossible when your mind isn't giving complete attention to something that demands attention. I want to learn about *myself* —not through somebody else's eyes, whether it is Christ, Buddha, or the latest guru. I want to learn—*the mind must learn* about itself, so it says, 'How am I to learn?'—which means I must observe. How can I observe when there is so much prejudice? There are thousands of prejudices that I have. How can I observe?

Then the next thing is, there is nobody to answer how the mind is to be free of prejudice. It must be—you follow?—otherwise I can't observe; the mind can't observe and therefore can't learn. So how is the mind to be free of prejudice?

Q: When I see something in myself I don't like, that is a fact, not a prejudice.

K: Madam, you have a prejudice, haven't you? All of us have some kind of pre-judgments—that is what it means, prejudging something. How is the mind to be free of prejudice, bigotry, conclusions? Nobody is going to answer me, so I have to find out. I can't just squirm under the question; I have to answer it for myself. Life demands it.

Q: By seeing the falseness of it.

K: You see the falseness of prejudice, don't you? But you are still prejudiced, aren't you?

Answer that question for yourself. How is the mind to be free of prejudice, a conclusion, an image that I have built about you? Do listen. I have built an image about you because you are a Christian and I am a Hindu, or I am a communist and you are something else. Now, how is the mind to be free of that image it has built, or that the culture has built, or that society has built, which has been implanted in the mind? How is that image to be put away? That is the question. Don't answer something else. The image is there. How is it to break down, so I'm free of it?

K: Look, I have been brought up as a brahmin in India, and I say I am that. That is a deep-rooted prejudice, brought about historically, culturally, and tradition says I am that. That is my conditioning. Is it possible for the mind to be aware of that conditioning? Just only that. No more. When it is aware of that conditioning, what takes place?

Q: It is no longer conditioned.

K: Are you saying this as an actuality or a verbal statement? When you are aware of that conditioning, are you trying to overcome it, change it, control it, or break through it? Or are you merely aware of it?

Q: I am just aware of it.

K: Now, what takes place then?

Q: I become free from it.

K: Wait. Either you are, or you are not. You can't say, 'I become'.

Q: If you like.

K: Not what *I* like, please. It isn't a game of what you and I like. The mind becomes aware that it is a Christian, a communist, a Hindu, and so on. That is its conditioning. In becoming aware of that conditioning, what takes place?

Q: Change.

K: No. I have to find out what I mean by *aware*, what I mean by *observing that conditioning.* Is the observer different from the conditioning? The mind is aware, or observes, that it is conditioned. Is the observer different from the conditioning? What do you say? There is nobody to answer you. How will you find out? Is the thinker different from the thought, from the conditioning, or is the thinker the thought and the conditioning?

Q: Do you realize your conditioning when you see that it is part of the mind?

K: Yes, sir, I understand. I am asking a little more. I am asking— we are asking—when you say, 'I am conditioned', is the 'I' who says 'I am conditioned' different from the conditioning?

Q: Certainly not.

K: Certainly not. So the observer is the observed. Now, wait a minute. Stay there for a few minutes. The observer is the observed. Then what takes place?

Q: I have learned what that thing is.

K: Then I have learned—you are saying—what actually is. Is there a learning about 'what is'? I must stick to this one thing, sir, sorry. The observer is the observed—right? We see that. That is, the conditioning and the observer who watches that conditioning are both the same. Both are conditioned. That means there is no division between the observer and the observed. Which means there is no division between the experiencer and the experienced, no division between the thinker and the thought; they are one. Right? Then what takes place? Take time. Go slowly. When there is a division between the observer and the observed, there is conflict—right?—trying to overcome it, trying to change it, trying to control it, and so on, and so on. Now, when the observer is the observed, there is no control, no suppression; there is no move to overcome it; there is only actually what is, only the observer is the observed, the image is the observer. Now what takes place?

Q: Duality comes to an end.

K: Sir, duality has come to an end when you say the observer is the observed. Duality exists, and the expression of that duality is conflict. When there is no conflict between the observer and the observed, what takes place? There is nobody to tell you, you understand?

Q: You have immediate action.

K: Wait, go slowly, go slowly. What takes place?

Q: I am not different from what I am looking at.

K: Therefore what happens?

Q: Conflict has ceased.

K: Yes, sir, we have said that. When the observer is the observed, conflict ceases. That is the greatest thing, isn't it? Conflict ceases. Has conflict ceased with you when you realize that the observer is the observed? Until that conflict ceases, you don't see the reality that the observer is the observed; it is just words. The moment you see the reality of it, conflict has come to an end, the 'me' and the 'not me'. The 'me' is the 'you'.

So what takes place when there is no conflict, which means when the observer is the observed?

Have you ever meditated? I see several of you sitting under the various trees with great attention. Have you ever meditated? *This* is meditation. You understand, sirs? This is the greatest meditation, to come upon this extraordinary thing, which is to discover for oneself—for the mind to discover for itself—that the observer is the observed. Therefore there is no conflict—which does not mean just vegetating, just doing nothing. On the contrary.

So I have to find out what takes place when the mind realizes that the image and the observer of that image are the same. And it has come to that point because it has investigated. It hasn't just said it, *that is so*. It has gone into itself. It sees that in learning, observing, there must be no prejudice. It sees that prejudice is an image and asks if that image is different from the observer. All that is an inquiry. It is an inquiry in which there is attention; therefore that inquiry brings about the realization that the observer is the observed, and therefore the mind is tremendously alive; it isn't a dead mind. It is an original, unspoiled mind.

Then what takes place? It realizes that the word *Hindu* and the maker of that word are the same. So is the image, the conditioning, there? Don't say no or yes. Is it there? The mind is conditioned as a Catholic. When the mind says, 'I am a Catholic', the 'I' is different from that which has been called Catholic—that is its conditioning. The observer says, 'I am different from my conditioning', and then he battles because he says, 'I must control', 'I must be generous', 'I must be peaceful', 'I mustn't kill, but I will kill when necessary', and so on, and so on. He plays a game with himself all the time. So when the observer realizes that he is not different from the thing that he sees, that *that* is the conditioning and that therefore the whole thing is conditioned, the whole structure is conditioned, then what takes place?

When there is an image, a prejudice, a conclusion, there is activity, right? If I am a Christian, I must resist everybody who is not a Christian; if I am a communist, I will convert everybody to my ideology. There is activity going on, isn't there? There is the activity of the observer trying to convince others, to proselytize, threaten. When the observer is the observed, all such activity ceases, doesn't it? So what takes place? There is complete immobility, isn't there? Oh, you don't see the beauty of this.

Watch it. When the mind is prejudiced, it is in movement. If I am prejudiced against you because you have hurt me, I resist—that is a movement. The image that I have built about you is the movement of a prejudice against you. I am a communist, and my education is to resist everything else and to bring everybody to that. So having an image indicates a movement from this to that or to change this to that—thesis, antithesis, and produce synthesis. It is a constant movement of the image, the word, the conclusion. So when the mind realizes, sees that the observer is the observed—*sees*, not just verbally accepts some idiotic idea but actually realizes it in his guts, blood, heart, mind—it sees that there is no division. Therefore this movement of the mind comes to an end. The movement of the conditioning comes to an end.

So there is complete immobility of the mind, which doesn't mean it is a dead mind. It doesn't mean a mind that has gone to sleep; it is a mind that is tremendously alive. It is alive because it is not moving in conditioned areas. So what takes place when there is complete non-movement?

It really is the most extraordinary thing one has discovered, if you have come upon it. That is, all movement is time, and time is thought. Thought is conditioned, and when thought operates, it can only operate within the field of that conditioning. I am Catholic, Protestant, communist, socialist, right wing, left wing, or centre, I am a Buddhist, I am nothing, or I must be something—all that is within the area of the known; the movement is in time, is time. Movement is time. Now, when the observer is the observed, there is no movement at all, there is only the observed. And when there is no movement at all about the observed, 'what is', what has happened? There is no movement, no chattering, no movement from the unconscious to the conscious, no movement at all. Therefore the mind sees, has the energy to look at, 'what is'. When there is a movement away from 'what is', there is desire to change it, control it, transform it. When there is no movement at all, it has the extraordinary energy to observe 'what is'.

And what is there? Another series of words?

It isn't an actuality to you; it is just a verbal acceptance. You don't say, 'Well, I am going to look at this, put my energy into this. I am dedicated; I want to find out'. And you can only find out when you have totally discarded everything that others have said.

Unless you do this, you cannot learn. You will repeat what others have said, which you are doing. And what others have said may be utterly silly, may be true, or may be false. Others have no meaning in this. It has meaning when the doctor tells you from his knowledge to take a pill or that you have cancer and you must do something. That's different. But here I know nothing; I have to learn. Learning means to observe. There is no observation when there is the movement of the image—do you see the beauty of it?—the movement of the image means the conditioning, and the movement of the conditioning. And that movement of the conditioning is time. And thought is time. So thought divides itself as the observer and the observed, and there is conflict. And this is the movement of our culture, of our religious activity, the conflict between 'what is' and 'what should be', between the observer and the observed. But when there is the realization that the observer is the observed, then the movement of the conditioning comes to an end, because there is no movement. Such a mind has come to it through meditation, inquiry, looking, asking itself, not anybody else. It has to stand completely alone, which doesn't mean being isolated, sitting still, becoming a hermit. On the contrary, the mind empties itself of its conditioning; therefore there is no movement of conditioning, therefore no movement of time. Then there is no 'what is'; there is only something entirely different.

❖

Q: Sir, all of this sounds so dreary to me because I can't do anything except pay lip service to you and follow you.

K: Then don't pay lip service.

Q: I can't get beyond observer and observed.

K: Then take time, go into it. Sir, you don't say that when you are hungry. When you are lustful, you don't say . . . When the house is burning, you want to act. And you act when you have pain, when you have a toothache. When you have some disease, you don't just play around.

Brockwood Park, 31 August 1978

Krishnamurti: What is learning, and can one learn through relationship? May we go into that?

What do we mean by learning? I think this is a fairly important question if we could go into it rather slowly and carefully. We learn from books, we learn from parents, colleges, universities, and we also learn through experience. We learn through various forms of events, which all become knowledge. That is fairly clear. We gather information, experience from various forms of events and incidents that happen in our life, and from all these we accumulate knowledge, and from that knowledge we act. That is one way of learning.

I CAN ACCUMULATE knowledge about science, about technology, medicine, and so on, and then act from that accumulation. Or I can act and through that action learn. Learning a great deal through action also becomes knowledge. So both are the same essentially: acquire knowledge and then act, or act and from that action accumulate knowledge. Both tend to become mechanical. If this is clear, then the question is: is there a way of learning that is non-mechanistic? To find that out, one must be very, very clear in oneself about the mechanistic activity of accumulated knowledge and the whole movement of that.

Please, as we are talking over together, find out how you learn and whether this learning is becoming more and more mechanistic. You hear me, the speaker, you read it, listen to tapes, learn, accumulate knowledge, and then say, 'Well, I am going to practise that'. Therefore that practice becomes mechanical. Now, we are asking: is there a different movement that is not mechanistic, that is also learning but is not accumulating knowledge and acting from that?

Questioner: Isn't it also mechanistic to accumulate knowledge to destroy the knowledge that you have accumulated?

K: Yes, it is still mechanistic. You try to get rid of that past knowledge that you accumulated, and you say that is not the way to learn, so you learn in a different form but yet accumulate.

The accumulation process goes on all the time. We are asking, please, if there is a different way of learning that is not mechanistic, that is not all the time functioning on the past movement. We are going to find that out. Do please inquire, question, challenge for yourself, and find out.

We said very clearly that action and then knowledge, or knowledge and action, are both essentially the same. Now we are asking: Is there a different learning? Don't jump to conclusions; don't say 'spontaneity'; don't say 'intuition'. Let's not be caught in words. Is there a way of learning that is not mechanistic?

Q: Does silence come into this?

K: You see, you are jumping. Start as though you don't know. We are starting with a question mark; therefore you don't know, so don't say it is silence, this or that. You really don't know. Yes, sir, that is the way to find out! With a clean slate you don't know, so you are going to find out.

Are you quite sure you don't know? Or you pretend you don't know? No, please, I am talking of oneself seriously. Do I pretend that I don't know, or do I actually not know another way of learning? Perhaps learning then has a different meaning: a way of learning that is not mechanistic. I don't know. I have to be terribly honest with myself; then I can find out. But if I say, 'Yes, I don't know, but I have a few ideas about it, behind me', then I am not inquiring at all.

Can we start by honestly saying, 'I really don't know'? It is rather difficult, because when you don't know you are looking, you are trying to find out if you know. When I say, 'I don't know', there is always the desire to find out, or I expect to be told, or I project some hidden hope and that becomes an idea and I say, 'Yes, I begin to capture it'. So can you be free of all that and say, 'I actually do not know'? Then you are curious, you are really curious, like a young boy or a girl learning for the first time.

Do watch yourself. Don't look at me or anyone else; watch yourself. That is, when you say, 'I really don't know', what has taken place? Your mind is not actively thinking about how to find out. Say, for instance, I really don't know, which means I have no hope of finding it, I have no conclusion, I have no motive. This is very important. When I say I don't know, in that is implied having no motive whatsoever. Because motive gives a direction, and then I have lost it. So I must be very, very clear and terribly honest in myself to say I really don't know.

Wait, listen to it carefully. I really don't know—then what has taken place in my mind? Find out; don't answer quickly. Hasn't it broken away from the old mechanistic tradition? When I say I really don't know, haven't I moved out of that field altogether?

Q: I don't think that one is thinking in terms of not knowing a new way of learning. All one knows is the conflict that mechanistic knowledge causes, just that. One doesn't know any more. And one can see that one doesn't know how to get over this conflict.

K: We are not talking of conflict yet, sir. We will come to that in a minute. We are talking about whether or not there is a different process of learning. If I don't know it and I actually say, 'I don't know it', what has happened?

Q: My mind then says that if I don't know it I am empty.

K: Oh, for God's sake! How silly people are.

Q: Why is it stupid?

K: I didn't say stupid, I said silly. Because we are not paying attention, it is empty. Is it empty? Or is it so tremendously free of the mechanistic that it is totally awake? Because it is intensely curious to find out? You see the difference? Wait, let me take an example. Do you know what God is? Of course, you have beliefs, you have dogmas, all kinds of conditioning, but actually you don't know that. You can invent something; you can think about it; you can argue for it, or be against it, but the actual fact is that you don't know. So you start with not knowing in order to find out.

Q: May I ask you, sir, do you always start with not knowing when you come to speak? Do you always start with saying, 'I don't know. Let's find out now'?

K: Yes, that is what I am saying.

Q: Is that what you do when you come here to speak? Is it what you do? Are you completely free of what you know before?

K: Please, I don't prepare talks. I don't do anything; I just come and I spill out. I have prepared talks, written them all out carefully, and so on, and so on, and one day somebody said, 'Throw away all your notes and talk'. So I did and began that way.

Q: There isn't a lot of difference, really, having it written down on paper and having it written down inside.

K: No. I don't. I am doing it now. Please! When you say actually you don't know, you stop the mechanistic process of learning, don't you? So your mind is not empty; it is free from that in which it has been functioning, and therefore it is now in a state of acute attention, learning. It is an acute state, free from that. Then what takes place?

Q: The mind gets bored.

K: Do try it, please try it as we are talking here. Do it in the sense attempt to find out.

Q: Inquiry.

K: Yes. What does inquiry mean? Inquiry implies that you must be free from your prejudice, from your habits, conclusions, from any form of opinion, so that your mind is free to move. In the same way, if you understand the whole nature of this mechanistic acquisition of knowledge and you put it in its right place, then you are free from it. And you are then capable of complete attention, aren't you? When there is complete attention, is there a learning? Please, this requires a little bit of going into.

I may be rather stupid this morning, so please forgive me if I keep on persisting in this thing. Perhaps we will come back to it a little later.

The next question involved in that is: can I observe myself through relationship? Can I know myself fundamentally, basically—all the reactions, all the nuances, the subtleties of myself—in relationship? That is the question that was raised. So we have to inquire into what we mean by *relationship*—the word itself. To be related is to be in contact, to be not only physically intimate but to meet at the same level, at the same moment, with the same intensity. That is relationship. There is a relationship between a man and woman, or one friend and another, or a boy and girl, when they meet not merely physically—but much more. When they meet at the same level, at the same moment, with the same intensity, that can be called a real, true, actual relationship.

Now, one's relationship with another is based on memory, on the various images, pictures, conclusions I have drawn about you and you have drawn about me, the various images that I have about you as wife, husband, girl or boy or friend, and so on. So there is always image making. This is simple; this is normal; this is what actually goes on. When one is married to or lives with a girl or a boy, every incident, every word, every action creates an image. Are we clear on this point? Don't agree with me, please; I am not trying to persuade you to anything, but actually you can see it for yourself. A word is registered; if it is pleasant, you purr, if it is unpleasant, you immediately shrink from it, and that creates an image. The pleasure creates an image; the shrinking, the withdrawal creates an image. So our actual relationship with each other is based on various subtle forms of pictures, images, and conclusions.

I am asking: when that takes place, what happens? The man creates the image about her, and she creates an image about him. Whether in the office, the factory, or any other field, relationship is essentially based on this formation of images. This is a fact, isn't it? Then what takes place? When she has an image and you have an image, there is division, and then the whole conflict begins. Where there is division between two images, there must be conflict.

Q: Why have images become so important?

K: First go into it step by step. Don't ask why. Do you have this image about your brother, your sister, your husband, your wife, your father? See that when there is the image, there is certainly a division: the Jew and the Arab, the Hindu and the Moslem, the Christian and the communist. They are all the same phenomenon; when that takes place, there must be fundamental conflict. The husband may go off to work, where he has created an image about himself, his position, his worth, his competitors; then he comes home and says, 'Darling, how are you?' and again he has his image, and she has hers. So there is conflict.

So it is a basic law that where there is division between people, there must be conflict. Full stop. The man may say to the woman, or the woman may say to the man, 'I love you', but that may merely be sensory love, sexual love. Basically they are not related at all. They may wear rings and hug each other and sleep in the same bed and live in the same house, but basically he is pursuing his ambitions, his greed, and all the rest of it, and she also. So basically they never meet at the same level, at the same time, with the same intensity. They cannot. Do we see this, not just accept the words spoken by the speaker—which is worthless—but actually see this is so in daily life?

Now, why do we create these images? Why do you create an image about your girl, or your wife, or your husband, or your boy? Why?

Q: Because we don't see the whole of the fact.

K: How can we see the whole, the whole beauty of relationship, the whole nature of love, when we are so concerned about our beastly little selves all the time?

Q: Is it because we are registering all the time?

K: I want to forget the registration. Look at it anew. Why do I—or why does one—create an image about another? Why do you create an image about the speaker?

Q: It is lack of attention.

Questioner 2: To be dependent.

K: Do look at it before you answer. See what you do first. If I may gently suggest, see the fact of it first, not say that it is this or that. Just see if it is so.

Questioner 3: We want to be recognized in some way or another.

Questioner 4: Is it because I'd like to know what is going to happen tomorrow?

K: Do look at it. You are married, or you have a girl, or a boy. This image-making goes on. And I am asking why. Take time. Please. You don't know; I don't know; let's find out.

Q: Familiarity; we take things for granted. We are at all times preoccupied rather than attentive.

K: I want to find out why I create the image about my wife. Is it habit? Is it convenience? Is it immemorial conditioning? Is it because of tradition that I do this, or is it in the genes so that instinctively I make an image about you?

Q: Does it matter why?

K: Find out. Is it this tremendous habit in which we live?

Q: No, it is influence.

K: Include influence, because one is so accustomed to being influenced, which is environment. Is it habit? Is it a tradition that has been handed down unconsciously from race to race, from generation to generation? Is it a thing that I have accepted as part of me, as I accept my arm or my leg?

Q: I think it is a continuation of the conditioning that we ourselves have received.

K: It is part of our conditioning, inherited from father to son, and so on and so on, generation after generation. So let's find out. Put all this together—habit, immemorial tradition, desire for a sense of nearness and yet withdrawal. Is that why you do it? Do look at it. Take a second, please, take a second. Or is it that we want to be certain of the girl or the boy, the husband—certain to possess her: 'She is mine and not yours'? All that is involved in it. The desire for certainty—it is my wife, my girl, my boy, my husband; I am sure. It gives me certainty in my relationship with another. 'I know my wife' is the most absurd statement. It gives me a feeling that I possess something and I am sure of that possession. So is it habit, a thousand million years of tradition carried from generation to generation to generation, the desire to possess, to be dominated—love to be possessed and love to be dominated, a neurotic state—and the desire to be certain—it is my house, my table, my pen, my wife? What do you say to all this?

Q: We should be free of all that.

K: We should be, or we are?

Q: We should be.

K: Oh! I should be on the top of the Himalayas, but I am not! How can we talk over together if we are not both moving in the same direction? Please. The 'should be' is non-existent; 'what is' is the only fact.

Q: Can one not accept this state by understanding it?

K: No, madam, we are doing it. We are doing it step by step, going into this. I am certain about my name; I am certain about my form, my physical form; I am certain I am qualified mechanically as a scientist, or professor. I am certain of my profession, my career in the military, or as a doctor. It is my career. I want to be certain in my relationship, and when that certainty is shaken, then begins the trouble; it ends up in divorce, or a separation, or whatever you like to call it.

So we create these images in order to be sure, certain, in order to possess and in that possession feel the power, the pleasure, the strength of that possession. And in this is man's inherited desire of a million years to hold somebody and not let go. These are the factors in daily life.

Q: So that implies something is just fixed, doesn't it?

K: That is right. I want to be certain. I want to be sure when I come back from the office that she is there. And when she comes back from the office, she wants to be quite sure I will turn up, too! This is the game we have been playing infinitely, in a variety of ways.

Q: Why do we need the certainty?

K: We are talking about something so tremendously serious. Knowing these are facts, not imagination, not ideas, not some conclusions that you have because I have talked about it, but daily facts, we ask if there is no possibility of relationship. You may sleep together, you may hold hands together, do all kinds of things together, but actually there is no relationship. That is a fact. And you don't want to acknowledge it, because the moment you acknowledge it, then doubt, fear, nervousness begin.

Can I learn about myself in my relationship with another? That is the question we began with. That is the question that was put. In that relationship I can observe my reactions: I like and I don't like; she said a nasty word; or it was so pleasant. I can watch my reactions. Those reactions are myself, aren't they? They are not separate from me. They are sensory as well as nervous, psychological responses. I am learning about myself tremendously as I go along. I have seen infinitely what I am doing, what I have done, what I will do tomorrow if I continue this mechanistic way of behaviour. And death comes and you say, 'Darling, I am leaving you'. She feels terribly lonely, miserable, unhappy, cries, finds out suddenly she is left alone, or he is left alone. And then he can't face it and goes off to some entertainment, or goes off with another woman, or whatever it is, or becomes tremendously religious.

What a game we are playing with each other. So I see this is a fact. I have learned a tremendous lot about myself in my relationship with another. Then the factor arises: can this image-making stop? Can this momentum of the past, all of that tremendous momentum with tremendous volume behind it, like a river with a great volume of water rushing, can all this image-making tradition and the desire for all that end without a single conflict?

Now, can this mechanism of image-making, not just image-making but the desire for certainty, the tradition, the whole structure of that, end? Are you asking that question? Or am I asking, putting my question onto you? If you put that question to yourself, do you say, 'I don't know, therefore I will find out'? Or are you already struggling to find out? How can this image-making come to an end? That means the ending of registration—not to register a word that he or she says, the slur, the insult, the nagging—not to register at all. Is that possible? I am asking this question; you have to answer it.

Q: No, it is not possible. I don't find it possible.

K: The lady says it is not possible; therefore she has shut the door.

Q: No, I haven't shut the door, but I find it impossible.

K: The moment you say it is impossible or it is possible, you have shut the door. It is like a man saying, 'I can't do it'; he's finished. I am sure, certain, clear each of us can do it if you put your heart and your mind into this question.

When the wife or the girl, or the man or the husband, says to you, 'You are rather stupid this morning', must you register that, react to the word, to his feeling? Can't you watch your own reactions to the word and his feeling? Can you watch all this instantly? Or if he says, 'You look very nice this morning'? Go into it. Is it possible not to register at all?

Please, we are talking about learning about oneself in relationship. We see why we create the image and so on and that there is no actual relationship at all. There may be physical relationship, but psychologically, obviously, you are totally divided. How can you be related and love another if you are ambitious or competitive? You can't. So you have learned a tremendous lot inquiring into this relationship. You have come to the point now when we say: can you hear the word, not shut it off, see the meaning of the word, the significance of the word, the expression on the face of the man or the woman who says it, and your own reaction to all that? Can you be aware of all that?

Q: Sir, it seems that we are continually getting into difficulty at this point by saying, 'I don't know'.

K: Don't keep on repeating, 'I don't know'. Then you are stuck. We started out by saying that we create these images and that why we create these images is fairly clear. And we said the next question is: can this image-making stop? Then I can say, 'I don't know'. Right? Because then the mind is tremendously alert.

Q: One has to be concerned to end the images.

K: Yes. You are concerned to find out whether the image-making can stop. If I say that it is not possible or that it is possible, then I am stuck. But when I say, 'I don't know', I am not static. I am moving; I am tremendously active and full of energy to find out. I am not transmitting my energy to you; you are doing it yourself. Please—that is a danger.

So is it possible to listen and not to register?

Q: Sometimes you are paralysed.

K: No, there is no paralysis, madam. You can't be paralysed when your relationship with another is so tremendously important. All life is relationship. It is not just you and I; it is a global problem. So we have to meet it globally, not just say, 'I love my wife'. 'You and I' is too little an affair. When you understand the global issue, then you will understand the little issue, but if you start with the little issue, you won't understand the global—global in the sense of the extent of it. It concerns every human being, wherever we may be.

So I ask: can I listen to the word, see the expression, the gesture, the contempt, the arrogance, and so on, on the face of the other and listen to it without any reaction? So now we will have to find out what we mean by listening.

Can I listen? What does it mean to listen? Do you ever listen? Are you listening now? Are you listening to what I am saying, or are you listening to a conclusion that you have made about yourself? Or, in listening, have you already drawn a conclusion? Or have you abstracted an idea from listening, and you are pursuing that idea? Therefore you are not actually listening. So are you listening now? That means you are listening without a single movement of thought because you are so tremendously concerned about this. If you are not, then you won't listen. If you are deeply, profoundly concerned about this, then you will instinctively, naturally listen. So are you listening from your experience, are you listening to the word and not to the content of the word, or are you listening and making an abstraction of what you are hearing into an idea, and saying, 'Yes, I have got it'? If you are listening without any movement of thought, any movement of intention, just listening, please carefully hear what I have to say. Can you so listen to the boy, or the girl, or the wife in the same way? You understand? Then you are finished. It is so terribly simple if you capture the simplicity of it. But intellectually we make a such a mess of everything.

So if there is the act of listening, then there is no registration. The other day after one of the talks, a man came up to me and said, 'What a marvellous talk that was. It was excellent. I feel as if I have got it all'. I listened to it very carefully. I have been told this for fifty years, and if I keep on registering how marvellous it is, I would be a cuckoo! So can you please find out, listen to somebody saying nasty things, or pleasurable things, so completely that there is no registration? Which means can you be so attentive at the moment the word is said that there is no centre that records?

Have you ever been attentive? Attentive in the sense of giving all your attention, all your energy, your heart, your mind, everything to that. When you do that, there is no 'me' from which you are attentive; there is only attention. In that attention there is no recording. It is only when there is inattention that there is a centre that records.

Q: Sir, there is no distraction.

K: No. There is no such thing as distraction. Please understand this. There is no such thing as distraction. You want to pay attention to that, and you are distracted, as one generally is. Which means what? You are not paying attention; therefore there is no distraction. So realize that you are not attentive and therefore distracted. The moment you are aware that you are inattentive, you are already attentive. Capture this, sir. There is no effort necessary in this.

So it is possible not to register at all. Can you live that way? Not for one day or a few minutes—can you live the entirety of your life that way?

Q: Excuse me, sir. When I am attentive in this way of which you speak, is the attention limited to the thing to which I am attentive?

K: No. Attention is attention, not limited to this or to that. I am attentive. *There is* attention.

Now, wait a minute; just look at it. The question was about learning and if one could learn about oneself through relationship. We went into the whole thing step by step, logically, reasonably, sanely. Now, just for a minute, listen to this. We went into it very, very carefully, in detail. Now, can you observe this as a whole thing, not broken up into little pieces? Can you have perception of the entirety of the structure? We have dealt with it bit by bit, fragment by fragment, or piece by piece; that means nothing personally to me. But if you capture the whole thing, then from that you can work out the details. But you cannot through details work to the whole.

Now, after taking this time, can you observe this phenomenon of registration, learning, relationship, as a whole? I mean by a whole having a deep insight into the whole thing instantly. You see, we are not used to that. We always go from one thing to another, from one fragment to another fragment, from one broken piece to another, and so gradually build up the whole—we think we have built up the whole—but the whole is not this. The whole is the perception of the whole structure and beyond. Then you can be terribly logical.

Q: And beyond the structure you said.

K: Oh, of course. The structure is very, very fragile.

Q: Does the attention include the structure and going beyond the structure?

K: Yes, sir, when we are attentive the structure is non-existent. When you are totally attentive, there is no structure. That attention is meeting the person at the same level, at the same time, with the same intensity. The other may not be; that is irrelevant. Your mind is meeting that totally. Then the objection of the other person begins, saying, 'You are indifferent to me', 'You are this; you are that'. You are not the cause of that.

Q: What is being attentive?

K: You are not attentive to something, about something, or for something; you are just attentive.

Q: Who, what, is it that is being attentive?

K: There is no you to be attentive; there is only attention.

Q: And there isn't another 'I' there?

K: No, please. See, you are going off to something. So after this time, are we free of the images? If you are not, you haven't been listening. And nobody can force you to listen; it is up to you. If you want the present kind of relationship with each other, and so with humanity globally, it is up to you. But if you want to find a way of living totally differently, it is also up to you, but you have to listen to everything in yourself, in others.

Q: I don't see how the structure disappears. I am sorry; I don't understand it. How does the structure disappear when I am attentive to it?

K: I will tell you. The structure exists with all that we mean by structure: that is, the desire for certainty, habit, centuries of tradition, and so on. All that is the structure, the picture, the image, which we have made about another. When we are totally attentive, there is no structure, and therefore you are beyond the image-making, everything. Just for fun, try one thing. The next time your wife, your husband, your girl, or boy says something pleasant or unpleasant, watch it. Just for that second, watch it. Be attentive for that single moment, and then you will see whether you are registering or not. You see, that is what I mean. Find out, try it; otherwise you will never find out.

Q: It seems to me there is contradiction. How can you watch it and be one with it at the same time? How can we be fear and watch it at the same time?

K: No, you are going off into something else. I am saying that you have listened for some time. You have realized, understood the mechanistic way of learning and a different way, and also whether one can learn about oneself through relationship. We went into that more or less. Now I am asking: can you be aware of this whole structure first? Be aware of it as you are aware of the colour of the dress of the person sitting next to you. Then be aware that you are separate from that, which is absurd. Therefore in that awareness you realize there is no division, and there begins to be a sense of great attention. In that attention—which is not yours or another's; it is just attention—the whole structure is non-existent. I say, *from that,* when your wife, or girl, or boy says something to you, be attentive at that moment and see what happens.

Ojai, 15 April 1979

W<small>HY IS IT</small> that we are not able to solve our own problems? Why do we seek out various types of analysts, psychologists, specialists, and ask them to help us? Is it because we ourselves are indolent, lazy, or we haven't the time, and we think we have time when we pay others to tell us what we should do? We have got into this habit, or into this conditioning of relying on others who have gone into a subject, have studied a great deal, know a great deal, thinking perhaps they will be able to help us. It seems to me we are always relying on others to help us to escape this trap we are in. The religions throughout the world have offered this. They are organized, excellently put together, with their rituals, dogmas, and so on, and we happily slip into that. And we are never able to resolve our own deep problems. We hand ourselves over to another; I wonder why we do this. It's all right physically; when the organism is not healthy, you go to a doctor, to a surgeon, and so on. When you want to build a house, you go to an architect. Perhaps the same concept drives us to go to somebody else to help us. We are never able to read our own book, our own history, because we are perpetually depending on others: group therapy, various types of psychosomatic treatments, psychotherapies; you know the multiplication of all that.

Wherever we human beings live, in the Far East, the Near East, and here, we are incapable of reading the whole story of mankind, which is ourselves. Is it possible for us to read this book that has been handed down generation after generation for many, many millennia, to read the story that we are, and not leave one chapter undone, unread? Can we read from the beginning to the end the whole movement of mankind, his evolution, both physically and inwardly, psychologically? If we are able to read this book, which is astonishingly entertaining—if I may use that word—fascinating, it opens the door to enormous possibilities. As we are the rest of mankind psychologically, if we know how to read this book, then perhaps we shall be able to alter the course of our lives. Because that is what we are concerned with—at least the speaker is concerned about that—to bring about a radical transformation of the human mind and so bring about a good society, a society where there would be order, peace, some kind of security, some kind of happiness, and go beyond all that, inquiring into that which is immeasurable.

We must learn how to read this book. So we must find out how to observe, not only visually but the whole movement of our consciousness, of ourselves, with all our complexities, with all our anxieties, fears, pleasures, joys, and the accumulated superstitions—the superstitions of the scientists, of the psychologists, of the religious people. We must find out how to read the whole thing, very, very precisely, clearly, and without any mistake. That's what we are going to do this morning, if we can: learn. Not that I am your instructor. Together we are learning how to look in this extraordinary book that is the self, that is the ego, the personality, the tendencies, the characteristics, the impulses, the inhibitions, all that which is our consciousness, and learning how to read that. To read it, one must have eyes and ears that are not dull, that are not blocked, that are not caught up in some kind of fanciful illusions, as most people are.

WE ARE GOING to find out if there is something beyond all this, not invented by thought but something actual, something that is not an imagination, not a thing put together by the mind or by the hand. We are going to read all that; to do that we must have clear eyesight to read this vast book that is ourselves.

Observation implies that there must be no distortion in our reading. Any form of distorted observation will prevent clarity of reading. Are we distorted? Is our perception, our inquiry, our observation, distorted? Please, we are asking each other this; I am not telling you it is, or it is not. We are asking, inquiring, exploring into this question. It is distorted if I have a motive in reading the book and want to change what is in the book. If the observation has already come to a conclusion that the end of the book must be this or that, if there are certain chapters that the mind doesn't like in its observation, or if it feels it must go beyond all this, all those factors bring about distortion. Obviously. So before I begin to read the book there must be clarity and great energy that puts aside any form of distortion. That is, if one is already caught in an illusion, which most people are, then our concern is not the book but why the mind is caught in an illusion, because a mind that is already in illusion can't read. Therefore my concern is why the mind is caught in an illusion. Is it fear? Is it that I may dislike what I may find, that I may be disappointed, depressed? Do I prefer to have my own illusions, my own concepts, my own conclusions about the book, and therefore I am incapable of reading it? So my concern then is to find out why this mind, which is inquiring, which demands that it should read the book, is caught in an illusion. Is it fear? The art of observation consists in giving thought its own place. Then the mind can totally, completely, absolutely be free from fear. Don't accept my word for this, but it is so. If you have gone into it, psychologically there is an ending to fear.

When the mind is caught in illusion, is it aware that it is an illusion? Or does it not know at all it is an illusion? If the mind doesn't know that it is living in an illusion, in a make-believe world, how is it to become aware of it? Suppose I am caught in an illusion. The word *illusion* is from *ludere*, to play—to play with ideas, to play with things that are not actual, that are conceptual. I play with a series of conclusions and beliefs that are not actual. If this belief doesn't suit me, I take another belief. I play with beliefs, and this playing is illusion. Because I cannot face what is actually going on, the mind invents beliefs, dogmas. Now, when I am aware of it, when I know I am in illusion, it is finished. It is only when I do not know that I am in illusion that there is no possibility of moving out of it. But the moment I am aware that I am caught in illusion, the very awareness dispels illusion. Obviously. So my mind then is capable of reading this book.

We are concerned with bringing about a radical transformation of the human mind, which has lived for millennia the way we are living: that is, with the quarrels, the anxieties, the violence, the brutality, all that is going on around us and in us. Such human beings can live only in disorder and can never bring about a good society, a good human being, and will never understand what goodness is. So we are doing this; we are inquiring into this.

Then what is this book, which is myself, which is yourself, which is the story of mankind? It is not only the story of mankind printed in books, the historical evolution of man, but also much more an unwritten book that nobody can ever describe or ever print in a book. This enormous evolution of which present man is the result is always moving, changing, modifying itself; it is never static. So my mind—one's mind—must be alert, clear to read this book. What does the reading of the book mean—the *reading*, not the book? The capacity to read is the capacity to observe, the capacity to listen to the story, the capacity to learn what the book is saying. Those three things are involved—the seeing, the hearing what the book says, and learning from the book. Are we doing this together? That is, are we together observing the book freely? Or are we interpreting the book? If I read the book but my mind is interpreting what the book says according to my desires, my wishes, my longings, my fears, my loneliness, I am really not reading the book but telling the book what I am, what I think is. So first I must learn the art—one must, sorry to use the word *I*—one must learn the art of reading, that is, the art of observing the book: that is, to observe, to see without the observer.

I'll go into it. Please have a little patience and go into it slowly.

The observer is the past. The observer is the accumulated experience. The observer is the result of all the influences, pressures, knowledge. With that knowledge, he is reading the book. Can we read the book without the past? It is not too abstract; it is quite simple. We think we know; we don't come to the book afresh. A schoolboy who goes to school for the first time doesn't know. He is fresh; he is young; he wants to learn. We must read the book in the same way; we must come to it with a freshness, not with all the accumulated knowledge that we have acquired, which is the book itself. So if you come to it, if you read it, as an observer who already knows the content of the book, then you are incapable of reading what it says. So there must be the absence of the observer; there is only reading, not translating what you are reading into your own peculiar idiosyncrasies, illusions, and desires. This is clear. So there is only reading, which is only observing the book.

Then, also, the book is telling you a great deal. Can you hear what the book is saying? Can you hear the song of the book? It is telling you something. It is telling you this enormous story. But you must be capable of hearing it, not only of reading it but capable of hearing this tremendous song of life that is going on. I can either hear with the ear or hear without the noise of the outside. I'll show you; I'm going to go into it a little bit. When you hear music that you really love, music that has meaning, depth, vitality, and beauty—not just modern 'pop' noise; sorry, you may like it, that's another matter—you hear it with all your being. You are absolutely with it. There is no division between you and it; there is no sense of remembrance of something that you have heard before. You are with the whole movement. When you hear the real beauty of Bach or Beethoven or Mozart, you move with it.

In the same way one must listen to the story that the book is telling you.

I hope you are following all this. If you are not, don't waste your time. If it's a lovely day, go and climb the hills, or play golf, or have a so-called amusing time. But you are here, so please give your attention, because it's your life.

And there is also the art of learning. This is a little more complex. When we go to school, college, university, we are learning, we are acquiring information, which is called *knowledge*, about various subjects, in order to have a good career, a good job. That is the accumulation of knowledge during a certain period of time, from childhood until you leave university, which can be used skilfully or otherwise. Whether you want to be a plumber, or a professor, or a scientist, or a mathematician, the whole process is the same: learn by accumulating knowledge and act from that knowledge. And there is also action and learning from that action. That is, accumulate knowledge and act or act and learn by acting; both are the same essentially. But there is another kind of learning that is a little more difficult. These two we know: accumulate knowledge and act; act and having acted learn from your action, which becomes the knowledge. Both are the same. We are saying something entirely different, because that is mechanical; that is a process of acting from the known. A conductor, a pianist, a plumber, a fiddler, a professor, a scientist, have all accumulated knowledge and act; therefore they are moving from the known to the known, modifying all the time. We are saying there is a different way of learning. This requires a little more thinking together.

One sees that the accumulation of knowledge is necessary to drive a car, and so on. If you want to build a bridge, you must know the stresses and the strains and the quality of the earth. That is, the mind has been informed, acquired knowledge, and acted from there. This is the everlasting movement of man: gather information and knowledge, then act. So the knowledge is the past. Of course. And from that knowledge you act. We are saying there is a different kind of learning that hasn't its root in the known. *In the known* means having knowledge and then acting. See the difference? I am going to point this out carefully. There is acquiring knowledge and then acting from it; so action modifies the knowledge, and the knowledge modifies the action. This is what we are doing all the time; therefore it becomes routine, mechanical, and there is never freedom to inquire into something that is not known, a freedom from the known to observe something you do not know.

For the speaker, the ascent of man does not lie in accumulated knowledge. Listen to it first; don't agree or disagree. First listen! Scientists and others have said man can only evolve by having more and more knowledge, climbing, ascending. But knowledge is always the past, and if there is no freedom from the past, his ascent will be always limited. It will always be confined to a particular pattern. We are saying there is a different way of learning that is to see comprehensively, wholly, holistically the whole movement of knowledge. Knowledge is necessary, otherwise you couldn't live, but the very understanding of its limitation is to have insight into its whole movement. You may never have thought about this. We have taken knowledge as natural, and live with knowledge, and go on functioning with knowledge for the rest of our life. But we have never asked what knowledge itself is and what its relationship is to freedom, what its relationship is to what is actually happening. We have taken all this for granted. That's part of our education and conditioning.

When you begin to inquire into the whole movement of knowledge, which is time, which is thought, you see the limitations of knowledge, for knowledge is always in the past and therefore fragmentary. You can add to it, take away from it, enlarge it, but it is always the movement of the past modifying itself, so in that movement there is never freedom. You may not have gone into this. This may be new to you, so please kindly listen to find out, not to agree or disagree. We are saying in that field there is no freedom for man. He may be able to have better bathrooms, better heating systems, and so on, and so on, but psychologically, inwardly, there is no freedom if the mind is constantly being driven or held by the past or is in bondage to it.

So is there a way of learning that is not merely acquiring knowledge? Is there a way of looking, learning, hearing that is not the constant accumulation of knowledge from which to act? Is there an action that is not bound by the past?

I'll put it another way. I have acquired knowledge—there is the acquisition of knowledge—and from that knowledge I act. In that action, that very action is limiting itself. It is not holistic; it's not the whole. There are regrets, all kinds of travail, in that action's coming into being. Now we are asking: is there an action that hasn't its roots in the past? Because if my action is born of the past, it is always limited; it is always broken up; it is never complete, whole. So is there an action that is free from the past? Just understand the question; then we can go into it. You may say that question is silly, that it has no meaning, but it has meaning when you see the whole complexity of knowledge and its limitation. The action that is born out of its limitation must be limited and confusing, and therefore out of this knowledge a good society can never come into being.

Is there action without the movement of the past? I say there is, which is to have an insight into the whole structure of knowledge. The insight is a deep understanding, a total comprehension of this whole thing: that knowledge, action, are limited, have no freedom, and therefore out of that there can be no good society. The perception of that truth is the release of a different kind of learning that is holistic.

Look, let me put it this way. What is the relationship between man and woman? What is relationship? As it is generally accepted, relationship means to be together in action. You earn a livelihood, and the wife remains home cooking or also goes out to earn a livelihood. Relationship implies all that: affection, sex, irritation, nagging, changing partners—if you don't like one girl, or one boy, you go to another. This process is called *relationship*. We are asking, what is actual relationship? Is there such a thing at all?

I am not saying there is; we are inquiring. There's no dogmatic statement in this matter. What actually is our relationship based on? Please inquire into it. You are related to somebody. Life is relationship, you cannot exist without relationship, but what is that relationship? You say it is *love*. One is rather shy of that word because love is loaded with all kinds of idiotic meanings and generally goes with the word *sex*. That love becomes mere sexual pleasure. When you go into the question of relationship, what is it actually based on? It is based, is it not, on the images that you have built about each other? Obviously. The two images have relationship. I know you may not like this idea, or this actual fact, but you have to swallow it, whether you like it or not. The fact is each one creates the image about the other, and these images have some kind of relationship. Each one goes his own way, with ambition, greed, separating all the time, perhaps coming together in bed. That's not relationship; it is superficial, sensational, pleasure. The image is actually the divisive factor between the two.

Now, the mechanism of this image-building is remembrance—remembrance of what she said, or what you said, the remembrance of your sexual images, the image of being kind, being angry, being nagged, and so on. You have built a great image about each other. It is the movement of thought that is the remembrance. We are asking if there can be a relationship without the image. That is the only relationship. If you see the truth of this, see that where there is image there is division, and that if you have an image about her and she has an image about you, the images keep people apart, if you see the full significance of this, which you can, then the mechanism of building images ends. Naturally, because all life is relationship, whether it is with nature, with each other. It's a relationship, but if we have an image about the heavens, the cosmos, the universe, then we have no relationship with life. You can have an image about nature; then the image is more important than the actuality. When you see the truth of this, the image-making comes to an end. Then there is a possibility of actual relationship with nature, with the universe, which is love.

So we are saying that there is a way of learning that is immediate action. It is not born out of knowledge; it is not impulsive action; it is not emotional, romantic action; but it is the action born out of the comprehension of the whole movement of knowledge, which is the truth of the limitation of knowledge.

Now my mind—*the* mind—is prepared to read. It is prepared to read the book without any distortion. Because there is no illusion, it is able to hear the whole story completely, without saying, 'I like or don't like'. It reads it like music; there is no part saying, 'I don't like that'. In learning from that book, in the very reading is action. Not reading and action, because if you do that, it becomes memory, and limited. I hope you understand this. It's marvellous if you go into it.

So the mind is prepared to read. And it discovers that the book is the mind. The book is consciousness. The book isn't out there on a pedestal for me to read; the book is this whole content of my consciousness, of your consciousness—greed, envy, this, that, and the other. The book is not there; the book is here. Then how will you read the book if it is here? We had thought reading is there, but the book is this, this quality of mind that is capable of such distortion, capable of such great technological events, capable of disorder, capable of great fears, anxieties, brutalities, violence, affection, joy, all that. So the book is this. So what am I reading? See what has taken place! Before I thought the book was out there for me to read, but now I have discovered the book is this thing itself. Therefore it can only read when there is absolute quiet observation in relationship. You understand? You are following this? It is only in relationship the book can be read. The relationship is my actuality—with my wife, my friend, my dog, nature, the hills, the beauty of a valley, and so on. So there is no conflict. I am not telling the book what it *should* be, so there is no conflict. If the book is me, there is the end of division, the end of escape, the end of inhibitions. The book is me, so there is no control; there is no desire different from the book itself. Then the whole movement of conflict, struggle, becoming better, trying to understand myself through a group, all that ends because the thing is there. Then you discover the whole movement in daily relationship. In that relationship you are observing, there is no conflict.

Talk with Students, Rajghat, 22 December 1952

YOU REMEMBER THAT we have been talking about fear. Now, is not fear also responsible for the accumulation of knowledge? This is a difficult subject, so let us see whether we can go into it very carefully and consider it. Human beings accumulate knowledge and worship knowledge. They think that knowledge is so important in life—knowledge of what has happened, knowledge of what is going to happen, not only scientific knowledge but so-called spiritual knowledge. The whole process of accumulating information gradually becomes a thing that we worship as knowledge. Is that not also from the background of fear? We feel that if we do not know, we will be lost, we will not know how to conduct ourselves, we will not know how to behave. So through other people's beliefs and experiences and through our own experiences, through book knowledge, through what the sages have said, we gradually build up knowledge that becomes tradition; and behind that tradition, behind that knowledge, we take refuge. We think this knowledge is essential and that without it we will be lost; we will not know what to do.

Now, what do we mean by knowledge? What do we know? What do you know when you really consider the knowledge that you have accumulated? What is it? At some level knowledge is important, as in science or engineering, but beyond that what is it that we know? Have you ever considered this process of accumulating knowledge? Why is it that you pass examinations? Why is it that you study? It is necessary at certain levels, because without knowledge of mathematics, geography, history, how can one be an engineer or a scientist? All social contact is built upon such knowledge, and we would not be able to earn a livelihood without it. That kind of knowledge is essential, but beyond that, what do we know?

Knowledge is essential at certain levels of our life in order to live. But beyond that, what is the nature of knowledge? What do we mean when we say that knowledge is necessary to find God, or that knowledge is necessary to know oneself, or that knowledge is essential to find a way through all the turmoils of life? Here, we mean knowledge as experience. What is it that we experience? What is it that we know? Is not this knowledge used by the ego, by the 'me', to strengthen itself? Say, for instance, I have achieved a certain social standing. That experience, the success of it, the prestige of it, the power of it, gives me a certain sense of assurance, of comfort; so the knowledge of my success, the knowledge of my having power and of my position, the knowledge that I am somebody, strengthens the 'me', does it not?

So we use knowledge as a means of strengthening the ego, the 'me'. Have you not noticed the pundits or your father or mother or teacher, how knowledge-puffed they are, how knowledge gives the sense of the expansion of the 'me', the 'I know and you do not know; I have experienced more and you have not'? Gradually, knowledge that is merely information is used for vanity and becomes the sustenance, the food, the nourishment for the ego, for the 'me'. For the ego cannot be without some form of parasitical dependence. The scientist uses his knowledge to feed his vanity, to feel that he is somebody; so does the pundit; so does the teacher; so do the parents; so do the gurus. They all want to be somebody in this world, so they use knowledge as a means to fulfil that desire; and when you examine, go behind their words, what is there? What is it that they know? They know only what the books contain; or, they know what they have experienced, the experiences depending on the background of their conditioning. So most of us are filled with words, with information that we call knowledge, and without it we are lost. So there is fear lurking right behind the screen of words, the screen of information, and this we transform into knowledge, as a means of our vocation in life.

Where there is fear, there is no love, and knowledge without love destroys one. That is what is happening in the world at the present time. For example, people have knowledge of how to feed human beings throughout the world, but they are not doing it. They know how to feed them, clothe them, shelter them, but they are not doing it because each group of people is divided by its nationalistic, egotistic pursuits. If they really had the desire to stop war, they could do so, but they are not doing it for the same reason. So knowledge without love has no meaning. It is only a means of destruction. Until we understand this, merely to pass examinations or to have a position or prestige or power leads to degeneration, to corruption, to the slow withering away of human dignity. What is important is not only to have knowledge at certain levels—which is essential—but to cultivate this feeling, to see how knowledge is used for egotism, for selfish purposes. Watch how experience is employed as a means of self-expansion, as a means for power, for prestige for oneself. You watch, and you will see how grown-up people in positions cling to their success, cling to their positions. They want to build a nest for themselves so that they are powerful, so that they have prestige, position, and authority; and they survive because each one of us wants to do the same, wants to be somebody. You do not want to be whatever you are, but you want to be somebody.

There is a difference between being and wanting to be. The desire to be continues through knowledge that is used for self-aggrandizement, for power, position, prestige. So it is important for all of us, for you and me as we are maturing, to see all these problems and to go into them, to see that we do not respect a person merely because he has a title, a name, a position. We know very little. We may have plenty of knowledge of books, but very few have direct experience of anything. It is the direct experiencing of reality, of God, that is of vital importance. And for that there must be love.

New Delhi, 17 February 1960

MOST OF US must be aware that a fundamental change is necessary. We are confronted with so many problems, and there must be a different way—perhaps a totally different way—to approach all these problems. It seems to me that unless we understand the inward nature of this change, mere reformation, a revolution on the surface, will have very little significance. What is necessary, surely, is not a superficial change, not a temporary adjustment or conformity to a new pattern, but rather a fundamental transformation of the mind, a change that will be total, not just partial.

To understand this problem of change, it is necessary, first of all, to understand the process of thinking and the nature of knowledge. Unless we go into this rather deeply, any change will have very little meaning, because merely to change on the surface is to perpetuate the very things we are trying to alter. All revolutions set out to change the relationship of man to man, to create a better society, a different way of living; but through the gradual process of time the very abuses that the revolution was supposed to remove recur in another way with a different group of people, and the same old process goes on. We start out to change, to bring about a classless society, only to find that, through time, through the pressure of circumstances, a different group becomes the new upper class. The revolution is never radical, fundamental.

So it seems to me that superficial reformation or adjustment is meaningless when we are confronted with so many problems, and to bring about a lasting and significant change, we must see what change implies. We do change superficially under the pressure of circumstances, through propaganda, through necessity, or through the desire to conform to a particular pattern. I think one must be aware of this. A new invention, a political reformation, a war, a social revolution, a system of discipline—these things *do* change the mind of man, but only the surface. And the man who earnestly wants to find out what is implied in a fundamental change must surely inquire into the whole process of thinking, that is, into the nature of the mind and knowledge.

I would like to talk over with you what is the mind, the nature of knowledge, and what it means to know, because, if we do not understand all that, I do not think there is any possibility of a new approach to our many problems, a new way of looking at life.

The lives of most of us are pretty ugly, sordid, miserable, petty. Our existence is a series of conflicts, contradictions, a process of struggle, pain, fleeting joy, momentary satisfaction. We are bound by so many adjustments, conformities, patterns, and there is never a moment of freedom, never a sense of complete being. There is always frustration, because there is always the seeking to fulfil. We have no tranquillity of mind but are always tortured by various demands. So to understand all these problems and go beyond them, it is surely necessary that we begin by understanding the nature of knowledge and the process of the mind.

Knowledge implies a sense of accumulation, does it not? Knowledge can be acquired, and because of its nature, knowledge is always partial; it is never complete. Therefore all action springing from knowledge is also partial, incomplete. I think we must see that very clearly.

If your mind and the speaker's are moving together in understanding, with sensitivity, then there is a possibility of real communion with each other. But if you are merely listening to find out at the end of the talk what I mean by knowledge, then we are not in communion. You are merely waiting for a definition, and definitions, surely, are not the way of understanding.

So the question arises, what is understanding? What is the state of the mind that understands? When you say, 'I understand', what do you mean by it? Understanding is not mere intellection; it is not the outcome of argumentation; it has nothing to do with acceptance, denial, or conviction. On the contrary, acceptance, denial, and conviction prevent understanding. To understand, surely, there must be a state of attention in which there is no sense of comparison or condemnation, no waiting for a further development of the thing we are talking about in order to agree or disagree. There is an abeyance or suspension of all opinion, of all sense of condemnation or comparison; you are just listening to find out. Your approach is one of inquiry, which means that you don't start from a conclusion; you are in a state of attention, which is really listening.

I would like to go into this problem of knowledge, however difficult, because, if we can understand the problem of knowledge, then I think we shall be able to go beyond the mind, and in going beyond or transcending itself, the mind may be without limitation, that is, without effort, which places a limitation on consciousness. Unless we go beyond the mechanistic process of the mind, real creativeness is obviously impossible, and what is necessary, surely, is a mind that is creative so that it is able to deal with all these multiplying problems. To understand what is knowledge and go beyond the partial, the limited, to experience that which is creative requires not just a moment of perception but a continuous awareness, a continuous state of inquiry in which there is no conclusion. And this, after all, is intelligence.

So if you are listening, not merely with your ears but with a mind that really wishes to understand, a mind that has no authority, that does not start with a conclusion or a quotation, that has no desire to be proved right but is aware of these innumerable problems and sees the necessity of solving them directly—if that is the state of your mind—then I think we can commune with each other. Otherwise you will be left merely with a lot of words.

As I was saying, all knowledge is partial, and any action born of knowledge is also partial and therefore contradictory. If you are at all aware of yourself, of your activities, of your motivations, of your thoughts and desires, you will know that you live in a state of self-contradiction: 'I want' and at the same time 'I do not want', 'This I must do' and 'That I must not do', and so on, and so on. The mind is in a state of contradiction all the time, and the more acute the contradiction, the more confusion your action creates. That is, when there is a challenge that must be answered, that cannot be avoided, or from which you cannot escape, then your mind, being in a state of contradiction, the tension of having to face that challenge forces an action, and such action produces further contradiction, further misery.

I do not know if it is clear that we live in a state of contradiction. We talk about peace and prepare for war. We talk about non-violence and are fundamentally violent. We talk about being good, and we are not. We talk about love—and we are full of ambition, competitiveness, ruthless efficiency. So there is contradiction. The action that springs from that contradiction only brings about frustration and further contradiction. Knowledge being incomplete, any action born of that knowledge is bound to be contradictory. Our problem, then, is to find a source of action that is not partial, to discover it now so as to create an immediate action that is total and not say, 'I will find it through some system, at some future time'.

You see, all thought is partial; it can never be total. Thought is the response of memory, and memory is always partial, because memory is the result of experience; so thought is the reaction of a mind that is conditioned by experience. All thinking, all experience, all knowledge is inevitably partial; therefore thought cannot solve the many problems that we have. You may try to reason logically, sanely about these many problems; but if you observe your own mind, you will see that your thinking is conditioned by your circumstances, by the culture in which you were born, by the food you eat, by the climate you live in, by the newspapers you read, by the pressures and influences of your daily life. You are conditioned as a communist, or a socialist, as a Hindu, a Catholic, or what you will. You are conditioned to believe or not to believe, and because the mind is conditioned by its belief or non-belief, by its knowledge, by its experience, all thinking is partial. There is no thinking that is free.

So we must understand very clearly that our thinking is the response of memory, and memory is mechanistic. Knowledge is ever incomplete, and all thinking born of knowledge is limited, partial, never free. So there is no freedom of thought. But we can begin to discover a freedom that is not a process of thought and in which the mind is simply aware of all its conflicts and of all the influences impinging upon it.

After all, what is the aim of education as we have it now? It is to mould the mind according to necessity, is it not? Society at the present time needs a great many engineers, scientists, physicists, so through various forms of reward and compulsion the mind is influenced to conform to that demand. And this is what we call *education.* Though knowledge is necessary, and we cannot do without being educated, is it possible to have knowledge and not be a slave to it? Being aware of the partial nature of knowledge, is it possible for us not to allow the mind to be caught in knowledge, so that it is capable of total action, which is action not based on a thought, an idea?

Let me put it this way. Is there not a difference between knowledge and knowing? Knowledge, surely, is always of time, whereas knowing is not of time. Knowledge is from a source, from an accumulation, from a conclusion, while knowing is a movement. A mind that is constantly in the movement of knowing, learning, has no source from which it knows.

Let us try another way. What do we mean by learning? Is there learning when you are merely accumulating knowledge, gathering information? That is one kind of learning, is it not? As a student of engineering, you study mathematics, and so on; you are learning, informing yourself about the subject. You are accumulating knowledge in order to use that knowledge in practical ways.

Your learning is accumulative, additive. Now, when the mind is merely taking on, adding, acquiring, is it learning? Or is learning something entirely different? I say the additive process that we now call learning is not learning at all. It is merely a cultivation of memory, which becomes mechanical; and a mind that functions mechanically, like a machine, is not capable of learning. A machine is never capable of learning except in the additive sense. Learning is something quite different, as I will try to show you.

A mind that is learning never says, 'I know', because knowledge is always partial, whereas learning is complete all the time. Learning does not mean starting with a certain amount of knowledge and adding further knowledge to it. That is not learning at all; it is a purely mechanistic process. To me, learning is something entirely different. I am learning about myself from moment to moment, and the 'myself' is extraordinarily vital. It is living, moving; it has no beginning and no end. When I say, 'I know myself', learning has come to an end in accumulated knowledge. Learning is never cumulative; it is a movement of knowing that has no beginning and no end.

Is it possible for the mind to free itself from the mechanistic accumulation called knowledge? And can one find that out through the process of thinking? You and I realize that we are conditioned. If you say, as some people do, that conditioning is inevitable, then there is no problem; you are a slave, and that is the end of it. But if you begin to ask yourself whether it is at all possible to break down this limitation, this conditioning, then there is a problem. Then you will have to inquire into the whole process of thinking. If you merely say, 'I must be aware of my conditioning, I must think about it, analyse it in order to understand and destroy it', then you are exercising force. Your thinking, your analysing is still the result of your background. So through your thought you obviously cannot break down the conditioning of which it is a part.

Just see the problem first; don't ask for the solution. The fact is that we are conditioned and that all thought to understand this conditioning will always be partial. Therefore there is never a total comprehension, and only in total comprehension of the whole process of thinking is there freedom. The difficulty is that we are always functioning within the field of the mind, which is the instrument of thought, reasonable or unreasonable, and, as we have seen, thought is always partial.

To me, the mind is a total thing. It is the intellect; it is the emotions, the capacity to observe, distinguish; it is that centre of thought that says, 'I will' and 'I will not'; it is desire; it is fulfilment. It is the whole thing, not something intellectual apart from the emotional. We exercise thought as a means of resolving our problems. But thought is not the means of resolving any of our problems, because thought is the response of memory, and memory is the result of accumulated knowledge as experience. Realizing this, what is the mind to do?

I am full of ambition, the desire for power, position, prestige, and I also feel that I must know what love is, so I am in a state of contradiction. A man who is after power, position, prestige, has no love at all, though he may talk about it, and any integration of the two is impossible, however much he may desire it. Love and power cannot join hands. So what is the mind to do? Thought, we see, will only create further contradictions, further misery. So can the mind be aware of this problem without introducing thought into it at all?

Let me put it in still another way. Has it ever happened to you—I am sure it has—that you suddenly perceive something, and in that moment of perception you have no problems at all? The very moment you have perceived the problem, the problem has completely ceased. You have a problem, and you think about it, argue with it, worry over it; you exercise every means within the limits of your thought to understand it. Finally you say, 'I can do no more'. There is nobody to help you to understand, no guru, no book. You are left with the problem, and there is no way out. Having inquired into the problem to the full extent of your capacity, you leave it alone. Your mind is no longer worried, no longer tearing at the problem, no longer saying, 'I must find an answer', so it becomes quiet, does it not? And in that quietness you find the answer. Hasn't that sometimes happened to you? It is not an enormous thing. It happens to great mathematicians, scientists, and people experience it occasionally in everyday life. Which means what? The mind has exercised fully its capacity to think and has come to the edge of all thought without having found an answer; therefore it becomes quiet—not through weariness, not through fatigue, not by saying, 'I will be quiet and thereby find the answer'. Having already done everything possible to find the answer, the mind becomes spontaneously quiet. There is an awareness without choice, without any demand, an awareness in which there is no anxiety, and in that state of mind there is perception. It is this perception alone that will resolve all our problems.

Again, let me put the problem differently. When we are concerned with the mind, we have to inquire into consciousness, because the mind is consciousness. The mind is not only intellect, feeling, desire, frustration, fulfilment, despair, but also the totality of consciousness, which includes the unconscious. Most of us function superficially on the conscious level. When you go to the office day after day from ten o'clock to five o'clock, or whatever it is, year in and year out, with a terrible sense of boredom, you are functioning automatically, like a machine, in the upper layers of consciousness. You have learned a trade or a profession, and your conscious mind is functioning at that level, while below there is the unconscious mind. Consciousness is like a deep, wide, swift-flowing river. On the surface many things are happening, and there are many reflections, but that is obviously not the whole river. The river is a total thing; it includes what is below as well as what is above. It is the same with consciousness, but very few of us know what is taking place below. Most of us are satisfied if we can live fairly well, with some security and a little happiness on the surface. As long as we have a little food and shelter, a little puja, little gods, and little joys, our playing around on the surface is good enough for us. Because we are so easily satisfied, we never inquire into the depths, and perhaps the depths are stronger, more powerful, more urgent in their demands than what is happening on top. So there is a contradiction between what is transpiring on the surface and what is going on below. Most of us are aware of this contradiction only when there is a crisis, because the surface mind has so completely adjusted itself to the environment. The surface mind has acquired the new Western culture, with its parliamentarianism, and all that business, but down below there is still the ancient residue, the racial instincts, the silent motivations that are constantly demanding, urging. These things are so deep down that we do not ordinarily feel them, and we do not inquire into them because we have no time. Hints of them are often projected into the conscious mind as dreams.

So the mind is that whole thing, but most of us are content to do no more than function on the surface. It is only in moments of great crisis that we are aware of this deep contradiction within ourselves, and then we want to escape from it, so we go to the temple, to a guru, or we turn on the radio, or do something else. All escapes, whether through God or through the radio, are fundamentally the same.

There is, then, a contradiction in consciousness, and any effort to resolve that contradiction or to escape from it places a further limitation on consciousness. I am talking about the same thing all the time in different ways. We are concerned with the mind and how the mind, being educated in knowledge, in the partial, is to be aware of the total. It is only when the mind is aware of the total that there is a comprehension in which the problem ceases.

All thinking is limited, because thinking is the response of memory—memory as experience, memory as the accumulation of knowledge—and it is mechanistic. Being mechanistic, thinking will not solve our problems. This does not mean that we must stop thinking. But an altogether new factor is necessary. We have tried various methods and systems, various ways—the political way, the religious way—and they have all failed. Man is still in misery, he is still groping, seeking in the torture of despair, and there is seemingly no end to his sorrow. So there must be a totally new factor that is not recognizable by the mind.

Surely, the mind is the instrument of recognition, and anything that the mind recognizes is already known; therefore it is not the new. It is still within the field of thought, of memory, and hence mechanistic. So the mind must be in a state where it perceives without the process of recognition.

Now, what is that state? It has nothing to do with thought; it has nothing to do with recognition. Recognition and thought are mechanistic. It is, if I may put it this way, a state of perception and nothing else: that is, a state of being.

Most of us are petty people, with very shallow minds, and the thinking of a narrow, shallow mind can only lead to further misery. A shallow mind cannot make itself deep; it will always be shallow, petty, envious. What it can do is realize the fact that it is shallow and not make an effort to alter it. The mind sees that it is conditioned and has no urge to change that conditioning, because it understands that any compulsion to change is the result of knowledge, which is partial. Therefore it is in a state of perception. It is perceiving what is. But generally what happens? Being envious, the mind exercises thought to get rid of envy, thereby creating the opposite as non-envy, but it is still within the field of thought. Now, if the mind perceives the state of envy without condemning or accepting it and without introducing the desire to change, then it is in a state of perception, and that very perception brings about a new movement, a new element, a totally different quality of being.

You see, words, explanations, and symbols are one thing, and being is something entirely different. Here we are not concerned with words; we are concerned with being—being what we actually are, not dreaming of ourselves as spiritual entities, the atman, and all that nonsense, which is still within the field of thought, and therefore partial. What matters is being what you are—envious—and perceiving that totally. And you can perceive it totally only when there is no movement of thought at all. The mind is the movement of thought, and it is also the state in which there is complete perception without the movement of thought. Only that state of perception can bring about a radical change in the ways of our thinking, and then thinking will not be mechanistic.

What we are concerned with, surely, is to be aware of this whole process of the mind with its limitations and not make an effort to remove those limitations, to see completely, totally, what is. You cannot see totally what is unless all thinking is in abeyance. In that state of awareness there is no choice, and only that state can resolve our problems.

Madras, 23 December 1964

LEARNING IS FAR more important than the acquisition of knowledge. Learning is an art. The electronic brain, the computer can acquire knowledge and can give every kind of information, but these machines, however clever, however well-informed, cannot learn. It is only the human mind that can learn. We make quite a distinction between the act of learning and the process of knowledge. The process of knowledge is gathering through experience, through various forms of impressions, through the impacts of society and of every form of influence. This gathering leaves a residue as knowledge, and with that knowledge, with that background, we function. Otherwise, without that knowledge, without all the technological knowledge that we have acquired through these many centuries, we cannot possibly function, we cannot know where we live, what to do. But the act of learning is a constant movement. The moment you *have learned*, it becomes knowledge, and from that knowledge you function. And therefore it is always functioning in the present through the past.

Learning is an action or a movement always in the present, without conformity to the past. Learning is not listening with one's knowledge. If you listen with knowledge, with what you have learned, then actually you are not listening; you are interpreting; you are comparing, judging, evaluating, conforming to a certain pattern that has been established. The act of listening is entirely different; it is when you are listening with complete attention in which there is no sense of conformity to a pattern, no comparison, evaluation, or interpretation—you are *listening*.

You are listening to those crows [in the trees over his head]; they are making a lot of noise; it is their bed-time. But if you listen with irritation because you want to listen to what the speaker is saying, if you resist the noise of those crows, then you are not giving complete attention; your mind is divided. The act of listening is the act of learning.

One has to learn so much about life, for life is a movement in relationship. And that relationship is action. We have to learn, not accumulate knowledge from this movement that we call *life* and then live according to that knowledge—that is conformity. To conform is to adjust, to fit into a mould, to adjust oneself to the various impressions, demands, pressures of a particular society. Life is meant to be lived, to be understood. One has to learn about life, and one ceases to learn the moment one argues with life, comes to life with the past, with one's conditioning as knowledge.

So there is a difference between acquiring knowledge and the act of learning. You must have knowledge; otherwise you will not know where you live, you will forget your name, and so on. So at one level knowledge is imperative, but when that knowledge is used to understand life—which is a movement, which is a thing that is living, moving, dynamic, every moment changing—when you cannot move *with* life, then you are living in the past and trying to comprehend the extraordinary thing called life. And to understand life, you have to learn every minute about it and never come to it having learned.

The life that most of us lead in society is to conform, that is, to adjust our thinking, our feeling, our ways of life, to a pattern, to a particular sanction or mould of a civilized society, a society that is always moving slowly, evolving according to certain patterns. And we are trained from childhood to conform to the pattern, to adjust ourselves to the environment in which we live. And in this process there is never learning. We may revolt from conformity, but that revolt is never freedom. And it is only the mind that is learning, never accumulating, that moves with the constant flow of life.

And society is the relationship between human beings, the interaction between human beings. It has established certain patterns to which, from childhood, we are made to conform, adjust, and in this conformity we can never be free. Society establishes a certain authority, certain patterns of behaviour, of conduct, of law. It never helps man to be free; on the contrary, society makes man conform, respect, cultivate the virtues of that particular society, fit into a pattern. And society never wants him to be free; it does not educate him to be free. All religions are part of society, invented by man for his own particular security psychologically. Religions as they are now organized have their dogmas, their rituals; they are ridden with authority and divisions. So religions too do not want man to be free. This is fairly obvious.

So isn't the problem that there must be order in society? You must have order; otherwise you cannot live—order being efficiency, order being that every citizen co-operates, does his utmost to fulfil his function without status. That is order—not what society has created, which we call order, which is status. Function gives status; function gives prestige, power, position. And in the battle of this competitive society, there are laws to hold people in order.

So the problem is, there must be conformity—to keep to the correct side of the road when you are driving—and also there must be freedom. Otherwise society has no meaning. Society does not give man freedom; it may help him to revolt, but any schoolboy can revolt! To help man to be free and understand this whole problem of conformity, to help him to conform and yet not be a slave to society, to conform to the norm, to the pattern, to adjust to society and yet maintain that extraordinary sense of freedom, all that demands a great deal of intelligence. Man is not free, even though he has lived two million years. Unless man is free, there will be no end to sorrow; there will be no end to the anxiety, to the misery, to the appalling poverty of one's own mind and heart.

And society is not at all concerned about this freedom through which alone man can discover for himself a new way of living—not according to a pattern, not according to a belief, not according to knowledge, but from moment to moment, flowing with life. If man is not free in the deep sense of that word—not in the sense that he is free to do what he likes, which is too simple and idiotic—but free from the society that has imposed conditions on him, that has moulded his mind, he can live for another two million years or more, and he will not be free from sorrow, from the ache of loneliness, from the bitterness of life, from all the various anxieties that he is heir to.

So the problem is: is it possible for man to conform and yet be free of society? Man must conform, must adjust himself— he must keep to the proper side of the road for the safety of others when he is driving, he must buy a stamp to post a letter, he must pay taxes on his income, and so on. But conformity, for most of us, is much deeper; we conform psychologically, and that is where the mischief of society begins. And as long as man is not free of society, not free of the pattern that society has established for him to follow, then he is merely moral—moral in that he is orderly in the social sense—but he is disorderly in the virtuous sense. A man who follows the morality of a particular society is immoral, because that only establishes him more and more in a pattern and makes him more and more a slave to it. He becomes more and more respectable and therefore more and more mediocre.

A man who is learning is understanding, as he lives, the whole function of society, which is to establish right relationship between man and man, to help him to co-operate, not with an idea, not with a pattern, not with authority, but to co-operate out of affection, out of love, out of intelligence. He is also understanding the heightened sensitivity of intelligence. And intelligence is only that heightened sensitivity that has nothing whatsoever to do with experience, with knowledge, because knowledge and experience dull the mind.

You know, you may pass a tree every day of your life. If you have no appreciation of the extraordinary shape of a branch, or of a leaf, or of the nakedness of the tree in the winter, or of the beauty of the sunset, or if you are not in total communion with the squalor, with the evening sunset, or with the reflection of the palm tree on the water, then your mind is a dull mind, however moral, however respectable, however conforming to society it may be. And such a mind can never be free. And it is only the mind that learns as it lives, every day, every minute, in the movement of life, of relationship that is action, only such a mind that can be free. The mind must be free, free from conflict, free from the self-contradiction that exists in man. The self-contradiction that exists in man produces everlasting conflict within himself and with his neighbour, and this conflict is called moral because it helps the human being to conform to the pattern that society has established.

Bombay, 21 February 1965

I WOULD LIKE to talk about something that may be considered rather complex, but it is really quite simple. We like to make things complex; we like to complicate things. We think it is rather intellectual to be complicated, to treat everything in an intellectual or in a traditional way and thereby give the problem or the issue a complex turn. But to understand anything rather deeply, one must approach the issue simply—that is, not merely verbally or emotionally but rather with a mind that is very young. Most of us have old minds because we have had so many experiences. We are bruised; we have had so many shocks, so many problems; and we lose elasticity, quickness of action. A young mind, surely, is a mind that acts on the seeing and the observing. That is, a young mind is a mind to which seeing is acting.

I wonder how you listen to a sound. Sound plays an important part in our life. The sound of a bird, the thunder, the incessant restless waves of the sea, the hum of a great town, the whisper among the leaves, the laughter, the cry, a word—these are all forms of sound, and they play an extraordinary part in our life not only as music but also as everyday sound. How is one to listen to the sound around one, to the sound of the crows, to that distant music? Does one listen to it with one's own noise, or does one listen to it without noise?

Most of us listen with our own peculiar noises of chatter, of opinion, of judgment, of evaluation, the naming, and we never listen to the fact. We listen to our own chattering and are not actually listening. To listen actually, the mind must be extraordinarily quiet and silent. When you are listening to the speaker, if you are carrying on your own conversation with yourself, turning out your opinions or ideas or conclusions or evaluations, you are actually not listening to the speaker at all. But to listen not only to the speaker but also to the birds, to the noise of everyday life, there must be a certain quietness, a certain silence.

Most of us are not silent. We are not only carrying on a conversation with ourselves, but we are always talking, talking endlessly. To listen we must have a certain sense of space, and there is no space if we are chattering to ourselves. To listen demands a certain quietness, and to listen with quietness demands a certain discipline. Discipline, for most of us, is the suppression of our own particular noise, our own judgment, our own evaluation. To stop chattering, at least for the moment, we try to suppress it and thereby make an effort to listen to the speaker or to the bird. Discipline, for most of us, is a form of suppression; it is a form of conformity to a pattern. To listen to the sound, every form of control, suppression, must naturally disappear. If you listened, you would find it extraordinarily difficult to stop your own noise, your own chattering, and to listen quietly.

I am using the word *discipline* in its right sense, its right meaning, which is to learn. Discipline does not imply, in the original sense of that word, conformity, suppression, imitation, but rather a process of learning. And learning demands not mere accumulation of knowledge—which any machine can do. No machine can learn; even an electronic computer or electronic brain cannot learn. The computers and the electronic brains can only accumulate knowledge, information, and give it back to you. So the act of learning is the act of discipline, and this is very important to understand.

We are going to go into something that demands the act of learning each minute—not a conformity, not a suppression, but rather a learning. And there can be no learning if you are merely comparing what you hear with what you already know or have read—however widely, however intelligently. If you are comparing, you cease to learn. Learning can only take place when the mind is fairly silent and listens out of that silence; otherwise there is no learning. When you want to learn a new language, a new technique, something new that you do not know, your mind has to be comparatively quiet; if it is not quiet, it is not learning. When you already know the language or the technique, you merely add further information. The adding of further information is merely acquiring more knowledge but not learning.

To learn is to discipline. All relationship is a form of discipline, and all relationship is a movement. No relationship is static, and every relationship demands a new learning. Even though you have been married for forty years and have established a comfortable, steady, respectable relationship with your wife or husband, the moment you have already established it as a pattern, you have ceased to learn. Relationship is a movement; it is not static. And each relationship demands that you learn about it constantly, because relationship is constantly changing, moving, vital; otherwise you are not related at all. You may think that you are related, but actually you are related to your own image of the other person, or to the experience that you both had, or to the pain or the hurt or the pleasure. The image, the symbol, the idea—with that you approach a person, and therefore you make relationship a dead thing, a static thing, without any life, without any vitality, without passion. It is only a mind that is learning that is very passionate.

We are using the word *passion* not in the sense of heightened pleasure but rather that state of mind that is always learning and therefore always eager, alive, moving, vital, vigorous, young. Very few of us are passionate. We have sensual pleasures, lust, enjoyment, but not the sense of passion. Without passion, in the large sense or meaning of that word, how can you learn, how can you discover new things, how can you inquire, how can you run with the movement of inquiry?

A mind that is very passionate is always in danger. Perhaps most of us, unconsciously, are aware of this passionate mind that is learning and therefore acting, and have failed unconsciously, and probably that is one of the reasons why we are never passionate. We are respectable; we conform; we accept; we obey. There are *respectability, duty,* and all the rest of those words that we use to smother the act of learning.

The act of learning is discipline. This discipline has no conformity of any kind and therefore no suppression because, when you are learning about your feelings, about your anger, about your sexual appetites, and other things, there is no occasion to suppress, there is no occasion to indulge. And this is one of the most difficult things to do, because all our tradition, all the past, all the memory, the habits, have set the mind in a particular groove. We follow easily in the groove, and we do not want to be disturbed in any way from that groove. Therefore, for most of us, discipline is merely conformity, suppression, imitation, ultimately leading to a very respectable life—if it is life at all. A man caught within the framework of respectability, of suppression, of imitation, conformity, does not live at all. All he has learned, all he has acquired, is an adjustment to a pattern, and the discipline that he has followed has destroyed him.

But we are talking of the act of learning that can come about only when there is an intense aliveness, passion. We are talking of discipline that is an act of learning. The act of learning is every minute, not that you *have learned* and you apply what you have learned to the next incident—then you cease to learn. And this kind of discipline that we are talking about is necessary because all relationship is a movement in discipline, which is in learning. And this discipline that is the act of learning every minute is essential to inquire into something that demands a great deal of insight, understanding.

Saanen, 4 August 1965

Krishnamurti: Someone pointed out that one wants to live in a different dimension, that one has perhaps felt a certain quality during these talks, or when walking by oneself in the woods, or when in relationship with some person, and said, 'If only I could maintain that and not slip back'. There is a contradiction between the experience, that feeling of a different dimension, and the actuality. If we can wipe away the contradiction, then we shall not have a moment during which there is a feeling of a different dimension and an attempt to reach it all the time. If we approach these questions and try to find out whether it is possible to eliminate this contradiction altogether, both at the conscious and at the unconscious levels, then perhaps we shall be living and not comparing. Shall we go into that one question?

How is one conscious of this contradiction if one is at all aware and sensitive? What tells you that you are in a state of contradiction? Do you become aware because someone tells you or because it brings pain? Do you want to pursue a pleasure, and in the very pursuit of that pleasure you become aware that there is a contradiction? Do you want to pursue one thing, yet your activity, your daily life pulls you away from it? One must find out how one becomes aware.

We are going into this step by step. We are not going to come to any conclusion. We are going to learn as we are watching, as we are examining, and therefore there is no conclusion at the end. Because if someone *tells* me that I'm in a state of contradiction, that has a totally different effect.

If I have an ideal of non-violence, of peace, and I am violent, there is a contradiction, or two desires pull in opposite directions, and there is a conflict. Life points out to me, or someone tells me, that I am in a state of contradiction. I may become aware of this contradiction through an effort, through a pain, through making an adjustment between the fact and the ideal. An incident or an experience tells me that I am in a state of contradiction. That's one state. Or there may be an awareness of this contradiction without any stimulus. Now which is it for most of us? Does an incident awaken the mind to its contradictoriness, or is the mind, without incident, aware of its own contradiction? Let's deal with the first now and come to the second afterwards.

We know contradiction through an incident, either pleasant or painful. I have an image, an ideal, a settled pattern of conduct, and some incident takes place that contradicts all that. Then I'm in pain. I say, 'I am in a state of contradiction', and nervously try to get over that contradiction, either by making the fact, which is my violence, adjust itself to the ideal, or by wiping away the ideal, leaving only the fact.

Through the established formula of conduct, or my own habits, there is an image of what I should do, what I must be, and then an incident occurs outside that image that contradicts the image. Because the contradictoriness creates pain, I want to get rid of it. I either adjust the fact, the incident, to the image, or I remove the image altogether and leave no centre at all.

Who is the entity that says, 'I must adjust the fact to the ideal', or, 'I must wipe away the ideal'? I have three things involved: the fact, the ideal, and the entity who says, 'I must get rid of the contradiction, either by wiping away the ideal or by merely accepting the fact'. Now I must find out who that entity is. As long as the entity exists, there will be contradiction.

Questioner: Contradiction is not connected with anything. Contradiction exists in itself.

K: We are coming to that presently. First, let's be clear on this point. There is the image, the 'what I should be', the ideal, and there is the fact that I am violent. I will wipe away that ideal that I have created and therefore deal only with the fact. Who is the entity that says, 'I must wipe away and deal only with the fact'? If I don't understand the entity, the centre that dictates, that centre will always be in a state of contradiction or create contradiction. Now, who is that centre? What is that centre?

Q: Isn't that part of yourself?

K: Yes, madam, but what is yourself? What is that?

Q: Something that stands in the way, that must be overcome.

K: Look, madam, we are asking ourselves what that centre is that says, 'I must not be in a state of contradiction, so I will wipe away the ideal in order not to be'. Yet the centre is still there, and we are asking what its structure, its nature is.

We are going to find out, learn about it afresh. That's the only way to learn. You may have thought about it, you may have come to conclusions about it, but if you have, you have stopped learning. We are now going to learn about the centre that creates contradiction, whether you wipe away the ideal or neglect the fact. The state of the mind that is going to learn about it must be that it really does not know what that centre is. We may have known it yesterday, but if we come with that knowledge of yesterday, we won't be able to discover what it actually is today. It might have moved; it might have changed; it might have transformed itself; it might not exist at all. So to find out, to learn about that centre today, we must be free of yesterday, free of the conclusions of yesterday. Therefore our minds must be silent, completely silent, still, with that question. Then we will be able to learn about it—then we *are* learning about it.

What is that centre that is always creating contradiction, the censor, who says, 'This is right', 'This is wrong', 'This I must do', 'This should be', 'I am not loved', 'I must love', 'I am unhappy', 'I must live in a different dimension', 'I have listened, but I have not got'? What is that movement?

Q: It is the movement of knowing.

K: It is a very difficult question we are asking. The ancients have said it is the soul, it is the atman, it is God, it is goodness, it is original sin. Do you mean to say that you are going to brush all that aside quickly and say it is this? First you must know what others have said about it and discover whether there is any truth in that. If you merely repeat what the theologians say, the people who believe in God, in truth, in the soul, in the atman, then you'll get nowhere. You are not interested in the repetition of some authority. If it is merely tradition, you throw it out. You investigate and come to a certain point; you come to it completely not knowing, silent. You want to learn about it; and to learn, you see that a complete quietness is necessary before you can look. Can you be silent without being forced and driven to be silent, be spontaneously silent, to find out what that movement is?

Q: I think that knowledge becomes the centre.

Questioner 2: Why have discussions at all? It becomes useless.

Questioner 3: It is in accordance with the principle of harmony.

K: I am afraid, sirs, you're not going into this question. You are merely stating what you feel, what you think.

Q: The mind is the centre of contradiction, the mind that has accumulated knowledge, the mind that has created images, the mind that has established a saviour, the mind that thinks that there are the permanent and the impermanent. The mind itself is in a state of contradiction.

K: Now, wait a minute! You have stated that. What have you learned about it? You have analysed it, felt your way to it, and said it is the mind. You have verbalized and made a statement. What have you learned? Have you learned anything? You say it is the mind that is in a state of contradiction, the mind that has acquired knowledge, the mind that believes, the mind that is the Catholic, the Protestant, the communist, the non-believer, the believer, the mind that creates the image. Is that an actual fact or an idea?

Q: Is it the unconscious desire for freedom?

K: No, madam. There is a statement made that it is the mind, mind including knowledge. What makes you say it is the mind?

Q: I have investigated.

K: I am asking you. One mind is asking another mind. How do you know that it is the mind? What makes you say it is the mind?

Q: We have been told.

K: You have been told? I have also been told that there is a marvellous world when I die, but I have to *live* in *this* world. When you say, 'the mind', either you have realized the fact—realized it as you realize hunger, and therefore the realization has validity—or you are merely speculating and saying that it is the mind. In that case you're not learning. So before any of us answer that it is the mind, the image, the conditioning, the pattern that has been established as a Catholic, as a Protestant, as a communist, we must learn about it, *learn*, not merely make a statement. Before we understand this particular issue, we must first find out what the mind is that is going to learn about it.

Look, my son, my sister, my mother, my grandmother, whoever it is, is not well, is unhappy, is not acting properly, and I am disturbed. From that disturbance, I want to do something—help her, hold her hand. But if I am disturbed, I cannot deal with the fact as a fact, unemotionally, unsentimentally, unstupidly. So it matters very much, when this question is put to you, how you are listening. Either you listen with a conclusion, with an idea that you already have about what that centre is, or you say, 'I really don't know; let's go into it'. If you really don't know, you come to the question with a fresh mind, not with a jaded mind that has already speculated, that is already conditioned.

So what is much more interesting than the issue, which in this case is contradiction, is the state of the mind that looks at it. If I look at a tree, what is much more important than the tree itself is how I look at it. What is the state of the mind when confronted with this question of contradiction?

Q: That is where the difficulty is, because it seems very plain that the mind has to be silent.

K: Be silent! *Be* silent! Be, be, don't talk! You see, you all talk, you don't do. *Be* silent!

Q: When you say, 'Be silent', you are trying to impress upon us the importance of being silent.

K: I am not impressing it on you. Look, I don't know Chinese. What do I do? My mind is empty; I don't know. I begin to learn as I go along. But you are not doing that.

Q: I think that if you watch your mind, in that same moment you get silent.

K: Madam, *be* silent, not *get* silent. Look, the issue is contradiction, why human beings live in contradiction. We said there is a permanent image established, a formula, and the daily fact contradicts that formula. If the mind wants to learn how to live without contradiction—*actually live* without contradiction—then it must approach with hesitancy, with silence, with quietness. And when it does, as I am doing now, there is the problem, and there is the mind that's completely quiet, not knowing about the problem. I ask what this strange quietness is, this strange stillness that is looking at the problem. Is it induced? Has the mind induced that silence in order to get rid of the problem and live in a state of harmony without contradiction, or is that silence natural? If it is natural, not induced, not made to be natural, then is there a centre? Is there a centre that is in a state of contradiction? The centre inherently *is* contradiction. And if there is only silence that looks at that contradiction, at that problem, is that silence a natural state, or is it induced because the mind wants to live in a state of harmony? If it is not natural, the contradiction begins again.

So can the mind approach any problem—life, the tree, the wife, the husband—completely with silence? This is one of the most difficult things to do, yet one sees that any other approach must breed contradiction. We have always approached the issue through positiveness: It *is* knowledge, it *is* the image, it *is* the mind, it *is* this, it *is* that—and so on, and so on. But this time we have gone a little further. We have said silence. Is silence the negation of noise, the negation of rumour, the rejection of this and that, in order to be silent? I must find out what this sense of negation is that is not positive, directive, but that must exist in life.

A really good mind is both positive and negative; it is both the woman and the man, not just the man, or just the woman. The Greeks had a word, and so had the Hindus. They symbolized it in their images and therefore have lost it. The moment you put it into words, into an image, it's gone. But if you begin to learn and keep on learning, learning, learning, you may then put it into words, but it will never die.

So we are going to understand a silence that is not the opposite of noise, not the opposite of this perpetual battle, and to understand that, one must understand the whole structure of negation.

Bombay, 16 February 1966

MAN, THE HUMAN being, has done everything to bring about a radical change, and yet, fundamentally, man has not changed at all. We are what we have been for two million years! The animal is very strong in us. The animal with all its greed, envy, ambition, anger, ruthlessness still exists deep down in our hearts and mind. Through religion, through culture, through civilization, we have polished the outer; we have better manners—perhaps a few of us have better manners. We know a little more; technologically we have gone very far. We can discuss Western and Eastern philosophy, literature; we can travel all over the world. But inwardly, deep down, the roots are very firmly embedded.

Seeing all this, how is one—you as a human being and I as a human being—how are we to change? Certainly not through tears, certainly not through intellection, not through seeking an ideological utopia, not through external tyranny—nor through self-imposed tyranny. So one discards all this, and I hope you have also discarded all this. To discard one's nationality, to discard one's gods, one's own tradition, one's beliefs, to discard all the things that we have been brought up to believe in, is a very difficult thing to do. We may intellectually agree, but deep down in the unconscious there is the insistence on the importance of the past to which we cling.

So the question is: how is a human being to bring about such a tremendous change in himself that he still remains in this world, functions technologically, and is able to reason sanely, rationally, healthily? Will—that is desire strengthened—does not bring about change. Will is the result of, is based on, desire, and desire is a part of pleasure. I need to change as a human being. What am I to do? I can see that exercising the will to control, to suppress, to have a drive—a positive assertive direction that the will gives—does not bring about this change. Because in that exercise of the will, there is conflict, and wherever there is conflict, obviously there cannot be a change. A conflict cannot produce a change. If you and I were in conflict about some issue, there is no understanding; there is no harmony; there is no coming together. At whatever level there is conflict, there can be no change. Change cannot be brought about through conflict, and the very nature of will not only is the product of conflict but also creates conflict.

YOU KNOW, THERE is so little beauty in our life. We have slowly become insensitive to nature. We are so occupied with our own problems, with our own interests and issues, our minds, our hearts, and our brains have become insensitive. We have accepted conflict as the way of life. And where there is conflict, there is no feeling. Conflict and love cannot go together. And yet the way of our life—in the office, in the temple, in the church, on the street—is a series of either casual or important conflicts. And if we would change all that, we must understand not only how to look at a tree, how to listen to the silence of an evening, but also how to live in a society that is so corrupt, which in its very essence is disorder. To understand all this, we must understand the nature of our thinking. Our brain is the machinery of thought, and that thought is the result of a great many experiences.

Before I go into this, please listen—not agreeing, because there is no agreement about this. I am not doing any propaganda; I am not trying to make you change into something else. If you are observant, you yourself will bring about this change. Please listen. As you are listening to those birds, as you see of a night the beauty of the sky and the quiet tranquillity of a rich river, in the same way listen, not intellectually, not merely to words, but to the implications of the words. Very few of us are capable of listening, because we already have our prejudices, our conclusions. We think we know. We are never learning.

To learn, there must be listening, and when you listen, there is attention. And there is attention only when there is silence. So to learn there must be silence, attention, and observation. And that whole process is learning—not accumulating—learning as you are going; learning *in* doing, not having learned and *then* doing. We are learning as we are going, as we are doing, not learning, then doing. The two things are entirely different.

Now what we are doing is learning in doing, because you are not being taught. There is no teacher or pupil. There is no guru. Because one has to walk by one's own light, not in the light of another. If you walk in the light of another, it leads to darkness. It is very important to understand that you are learning, and to learn there must be silence. How can you learn if your mind is chattering? How can you look? How can you attend? Look at a boy who is learning in school! If he is really interested in his subject, he is essentially quiet and giving his attention. From this attention he is learning. Even if he wants to look out the window, that very act, to look, is part of that learning.

So what we are doing is learning, and to learn there is no teacher who teaches. All one needs is attention, that sense of simple, quiet silence, and then one learns. Then, in that, there is no book, no teacher, no one to point out to you; the whole thing is happening.

So we are concerned with a way of life in which all conflict has ceased. We are going to learn, not ask, 'What am I to do in order to live without conflict?' That is the most immature, childish question, and the moment you ask it, you create the man who will teach you what to do, and therefore you are caught. You have to see that learning is in doing; whether there is a mistake or no mistake is irrelevant.

Learning is in doing, not in being taught, except technologically. Technologically, I need to be helped—to learn about an electronic brain, and so on. But here there is no one to teach you, and the learning has to begin. What another teaches is not truth. The follower destroys truth—as the guru does. So you have to learn, and learning is in doing. That is the beauty of learning. That learning becomes a joy, a delight, not boredom, not something that you have to do.

So to go into this question of how to live without conflict at all the levels of our being—intellectually, in our emotions, in our feelings, in our physical ways—we have to learn. Though the speaker may explore for you, you have to learn, and this means that you are exploring with him. Therefore learning is always together; that means learning is always a process of relationship. Please understand the beauty of this. You cannot learn by yourself. Learning is in doing, and the doing is in relationship, not withdrawing, examining, analysing, and then learning. Learning is an act of relationship, and relationship is life. And life is this tremendous movement of everyday existence that is relationship. And to find a way of living in which there is no conflict is the greatest discovery, the greatest way.

The first thing to realize is that conflict, however much it is part of our life, cannot possibly produce under any circumstances a life of deep awareness, silence, and beauty. A man in conflict cannot possibly love. An ambitious man has no love at all. How can he have? He is in conflict; he is being frustrated; he wants to fulfil; his drive is towards that. Therefore there is no beauty, no affection, no tenderness. He may have sentimentality emotionally, but that is not love.

A mind that has the deep realization that conflict in any form, under any circumstances—however much one is used to it, however much one has lived in it—destroys, perverts, has learned the implication of conflict and begins to learn a way of life in which there is no conflict at all. Yet it will be tremendously alive, will not go to sleep, will not become lethargic, inactive, dull, stupid. It is the man in conflict who leads a dull, stupid, insensitive life, not the man who is free from conflict.

But to understand and to come upon this extraordinary state of mind in which there is no conflict, one has to understand the structure and the nature of conflict and see actually, objectively, the whole business of it. Without seeing that, you can never go beyond it. It is like a man who talks about the beauty of life, listens to music, goes to the theatre, sees the trees of an evening against the setting sun, but does not notice the filth of the street. Because he has got used to the filth of the street, the dirt, the squalor, the poverty, he is not really a man who loves beauty. To love beauty, you must also be aware of the dirt, the squalor, the poverty, and the inhumanity.

Saanen, 12 July 1964

CAN YOU, AS an individual, really go into yourself very searchingly, ruthlessly, and find out if it is at all possible for each one of us to be completely free? Surely, it is only in freedom that there can be change. And we do have to change, not superficially, not in the sense of merely pruning a little bit here and there, but we have to bring about a radical mutation in the very structure of the mind itself. That is why I feel it is so important to talk about change, to discuss it, and to see how far each one of us can go into this problem.

Do you know what I mean by change? To change is to think in a totally different manner; it is to bring about a state of mind in which there is no anxiety at any time, no sense of conflict, no struggle to achieve, to be or to become something. It is to be completely free of fear. To find out what it means to be free of fear, I think one has to understand this question of the teacher and the taught and thereby discover what learning is. There is no teacher here, and there is no person who is being taught. We are all learning. So you have to be completely rid of the idea that someone is going to instruct you or tell you what to do—which means that the relationship between you and the speaker is entirely different. We are learning; you are not being taught. If you really understand that you are not here to be taught by anyone, that there is no teacher to teach you, no saviour to save you, no guru to tell you what to do—if you really understand this fact—

then you have to do everything for yourself, and that demands tremendous energy.

We generally learn through study, through books, through experience, or through being instructed. Those are the usual ways of learning. We commit to memory what to do and what not to do, what to think and what not to think, how to feel, how to react. Through experience, through study, through analysis, through probing, through introspective examination, we store up knowledge as memory, and memory then responds to further challenges and demands, from which there is more and more learning. With this process we are quite familiar; it is the only way we learn. I do not know how to fly an aeroplane, so I learn. I am instructed, I gain experience the memory of which is retained, and then I fly. That is the only process of learning with which most of us are acquainted. We learn through study, through experience, through instruction. What is learned is committed to memory as knowledge, and that knowledge functions whenever there is a challenge or whenever we have to do something.

Now, I think there is a totally different way of learning, but to understand it, and to learn in this different way, you must be completely rid of authority; otherwise you will merely be instructed, and you will repeat what you have heard. That is why it is very important to understand the nature of authority. Authority prevents learning—the learning that is not the accumulation of knowledge as memory. Memory always responds in patterns, so it has no freedom. A man who is burdened with knowledge, with instructions, who is weighed down by the things he has learned, is never free. He may be most extraordinarily erudite, but his accumulation of knowledge prevents him from being free, and therefore he is incapable of learning.

We accumulate various forms of knowledge—scientific, physiological, technological, and so on—and this knowledge is necessary for the physical well-being of man. But we also accumulate knowledge in order to be safe, in order to function without disturbance, in order to act always within the borders of our own information and thereby feel secure. We want never to be uncertain, we are afraid of uncertainty, and therefore we accumulate knowledge. This psychological accumulation is what I am talking about, and it is this that completely blocks freedom.

So the moment one begins to inquire into what is freedom, one has to question not only authority but knowledge. If you are merely being instructed, if you are merely accumulating what you hear, what you read, what you experience, then you will find that you can never be free, because you are always functioning within the pattern of the known. This is what actually happens to most of us, so what is one to do?

One sees how the mind and the brain function. The brain is an animalistic, progressive, evolutionary thing that lives and functions within the walls of its own experience, its own knowledge, its own hopes and fears. It is everlastingly active in safeguarding and protecting itself, and in some measure it has to be; otherwise it would soon be destroyed. It must have some degree of security, so it habitually benefits itself by gathering every kind of information, obeying every kind of instruction, creating a pattern by which to live, and so never being free. If one has observed one's own brain, the whole functioning of oneself, one is aware of this patterned mode of existence in which there is no spontaneity at all.

Then what is learning? Is there a different kind of learning, a learning that is not cumulative, that doesn't become merely a background of memory or knowledge that creates patterns and blocks freedom? Is there a kind of learning that doesn't become a burden, that doesn't cripple the mind but, on the contrary, gives it freedom? If you have ever put this question to yourself, not superficially but deeply, you will know that one has to find out why the mind clings to authority. Whether it be the authority of the instructor, of the saviour, of the book, or the authority of one's own knowledge and experience, why does the mind cling to that authority?

You know, authority takes many forms. There is the authority of books, the authority of the church, the authority of the ideal, the authority of your own experience, and the authority of the knowledge that you have gathered. Why do you cling to those authorities? Technologically there is need of authorities. That is simple and obvious. But we are talking about the psychological state of the mind; and quite apart from technological authority, why does the mind cling to authority in the psychological sense?

Obviously, the mind clings to authority because it is afraid of uncertainty, insecurity; it is afraid of the unknown, of what may happen tomorrow. And can you and I live without any authority at all—authority in the sense of domination, assertion, dogmatism, aggressiveness, wanting to succeed, wanting to be famous, wanting to become somebody? Can we live in this world—going to the office and all the rest of it—in a state of complete humility? That is a very difficult thing to find out, is it not? But I think it is only in that state of complete humility—which is the state of a mind that is always willing not to know—that one can learn. Otherwise one is always accumulating and therefore ceasing to learn.

So can one live from day to day in that state? Surely, a mind that is really learning has no authority, nor does it seek authority. Because it is in a state of constant learning, not only from outward things, but also from inward things, it does not belong to any group, to any society, to any race or culture. If you are constantly learning from everything without accumulation, how can there be any authority, any teacher? How can you possibly follow anyone? And that is the only way to live—not learning from books, I don't mean that, but learning from your own demands, from the movements of your own thought, your own being. Then your mind is always fresh; it looks at everything anew and not with the jaded look of knowledge, of experience, of that which it has learned. If one understands this really, profoundly, then all authority ceases. Then the speaker is of no importance at all.

The extraordinary state that truth reveals, the immensity of reality, cannot be given to you by another. There is no authority; there is no guide. You have to discover it for yourself and thereby bring some sense into this chaos that we call life. It is a journey that must be taken completely alone, without companions, with neither wife, nor husband, nor books. You can set out on this journey only when you really see the truth that you have to walk completely alone, and then you are alone, not out of bitterness, not out of cynicism, not out of despair, but because you see the fact that aloneness is absolutely necessary. It is this fact, and the perceiving of this fact, that sets one free to walk alone. The book, the saviour, the teacher—they are yourself. So you have to investigate yourself; you have to learn about yourself—which does not mean accumulating knowledge about yourself and with that knowledge looking at the movements of your own thought.

To learn about yourself, to know yourself, you must observe yourself with a freshness, with a freedom. You can't learn about yourself if you are merely applying knowledge, that is, looking at yourself in terms of what you have learned from some instructor, from some book, or from your own experience.

The 'you' is an extraordinary entity; it is a complex, vital thing, tremendously alive, constantly changing, undergoing all kinds of experiences. It is a vortex of enormous energy, and there is no one who can teach you about it—no one! That is the first thing to realize. When once you realize that, really see the truth of it, you are already liberated from a heavy burden: you have ceased looking to someone else to tell you what to do. There is already the beginning of this extraordinary perfume of freedom.

So I have to know myself, because without knowing myself, there can be no end to conflict; there can be no end to fear and despair; there can be no understanding of death. When I understand myself, I understand all human beings, the whole of human relationship. To understand oneself is to learn about the physical body and the various responses of the nerves; it is to be aware of every movement of thought; it is to comprehend the thing called jealousy, brutality, and to discover what is affection, what is love. It is to understand the whole of that which is the 'me', the 'you'.

Learning is not a process of laying the foundation of knowledge. Learning is from moment to moment; it is a movement in which you are watching yourself infinitely, never condemning, never judging, never evaluating, but merely observing. The moment you condemn, interpret, or evaluate, you have a pattern of knowledge, of experience, and that pattern prevents you from learning.

A mutation at the very root of the mind is possible only when you understand yourself. And there must be such a mutation; there must be change. I am not using the word *change* in the sense of being influenced by society, by climate, by experience, or by pressure in some other form. Pressures and influences will merely push you in a certain direction. I mean the change that comes about effortlessly because you understand yourself. Surely there is a vast difference between the two, between the change brought about through compulsion and the change that comes spontaneously, naturally, freely.

You see, I feel that our life is so superficial. We know and have experienced a great deal, we can talk very cleverly, but we really have no depth. We live on the surface, and living on the surface, we try to make that surface living very serious. But I am talking about a seriousness that is not merely at the superficial level, a seriousness that penetrates into the very depths of one's own being. Most of us are not really free, and I feel that unless we are free—free from worry, free from habits, free from psychosomatic disabilities, free from fear—our life remains terribly shallow and empty, and in that condition we grow old and die.

So let us find out if we can break through this superficial existence that we have so carefully nurtured and delve into something much deeper. And the delving process is not through authority, it is not a matter of being told by another how to do it, for there is nobody who can tell you. What we are here to do is to learn together what is true in all this, and once you really understand what is true, then all looking to authority is over. Then you do not need any book; you do not go to any church or temple; you have ceased to be a follower. There is a great beauty, a great depth, a great love in freedom, of which now we know nothing at all because we are not free. So our first concern, it seems to me, is to inquire into this freedom, not only through verbal or linguistic analysis but also through being free of the word.

IT IS VERY hot, but I am afraid we have done everything we can to make the inside of this tent fairly cool.

You know, one has to discipline oneself, not through imposition or rigid control but through understanding the whole question of discipline, learning about it. Just take this immediate thing, the heat. One can be aware of this heat and not be bothered by it, because one's interest, one's inquiry, which is the very movement of learning, is much more important than the heat and the discomfort of the body. So learning demands discipline, and the very act of learning is discipline; therefore there need be no imposed discipline, no artificial control. That is, I want to listen not only to what is being said but also to all the reactions that those words awaken in me. I want to be aware of every movement of thought, of every feeling, of every gesture. That in itself is discipline, and such discipline is extraordinarily flexible.

So I think the first thing you have to discover is whether you—as a human being living in a particular culture or community—really demand freedom as you demand food, sex, comfort, and how far and how deep you are willing to go in order to be free. That is the only thing we can share, that and nothing else. Because everything else becomes mere sentimentality, devotion, emotionalism, which is too immature. But if you and I together are really seeking, inquiring, learning what it means to be free, then in that abundance we can share.

As I said at the beginning, here there is no teacher; there are no taught. Each one of us is learning, but not about somebody else. You are not learning about the speaker or about your neighbour. You are learning about yourself. And if you are learning about yourself, then you are the speaker; you are your neighbour. If you are learning about yourself, you can love your neighbour; otherwise you cannot, and all this will remain mere words. You cannot love your neighbour if you are competitive. Our whole social structure—economic, political, moral, religious—is based on competition, and at the same time we say we must love our neighbour. Such a thing is impossible, because where there is competition there can be no love.

So to understand what love is, what truth is, there must be freedom, and nobody can give that to you. You have to find it for yourself through hard work.

Madras, 16 December 1959

I THINK IT would be marvellous if, without words, one could convey what one really feels about the whole problem of existence. Besides the superficial necessity of having a job and all the rest of it, there are the deep, inward urges, the demands, the contradictory states of being, both conscious and unconscious; and I wonder if it is not possible to go beyond them all, beyond the frontiers that the mind has imposed upon itself, beyond the narrow limits of one's own heart, and to live there, to act, to think, and to feel from that state while carrying on one's everyday activities. I think it can be done, not merely the communication of it but the fact of it. Surely, we can break through the limitations that the mind has placed upon itself, because, after all, we have only one problem. As the tree with its many roots, its many branches and leaves, is a totality, so we have only one basic problem. And if, by some miracle, by some grace, by some way of looking at the clouds of an evening, the mind could become extraordinarily sensitive to every movement of thought, of feeling—if it could do that, not theoretically but actually—then I think we would have solved our problem.

As I said, there is essentially only one problem—the problem of me and my urges—from which all our other problems arise. Our real problems are not how to land on the moon, or how to fire a rocket to Venus; they are very intimate, but unfortunately we do not seem to know how to deal with them. I am not at all sure that we are even aware of our real problem. To know love, to feel the beauty of nature, to worship something beyond the creations of man—I think all this is denied to us if we do not understand our immediate problems.

So I would like to think along with you on this question of whether or not the mind can break through its own frontiers, go beyond its own limitations, because our lives are obviously very shallow. You may have all the wealth that the earth can give you; you may be very erudite; you may have read many books and be able to quote very learnedly all the established authorities, past and present; or you may be very simple, just living and struggling from day to day, with all the little pleasures and sorrows of family life. Whatever one is, surely it is of the utmost importance to find out in what manner the barriers that the mind has created for it-self can be swept away. That, it seems to me, is our fundamental problem. Through so-called education, through tradition, through various forms of social, moral, and religious conditioning the mind is limited, caught up in a moving vortex of environmental influences. Is it possible for the mind to break away from all this conditioning so that it can live with joy, perceiving the beauty of things, feeling an extraordinary sense of immeasurable life?

I think it is possible, but I do not think it is a gradual process. It is not through evolution, through time, that the breaking away takes place. It is done instantly or never. The perception of truth does not come at the end of many years. There is no tomorrow in understanding. Either the mind understands immediately or not at all. It is very difficult for the mind to see this, because most of us are so accustomed to thinking in terms of tomorrow. We say, 'Give me time, let me have more experience, and eventually I shall understand'. But have you not noticed that understanding always comes in a flash, never through calculation, through time, never through exercise and slow development? The mind that relies on this idea of gradual comprehension is essentially lazy. Don't ask, 'How is a lazy mind to be made alert, vital, active?' There is no 'how'. However much a stupid mind may try to become clever, it will still be stupid. A petty mind does not cease to be petty by worshipping the god it has invented. Time is not going to reveal the truth, the beauty of anything. What really brings understanding is the state of attention—just being attentive, even for one second with one's whole being, without calculation, without premeditation. If you and I can be totally attentive on the instant, then I think there is an instantaneous comprehension, a total understanding.

But it is very difficult to give one's total attention to something, is it not? I do not know if you have ever tried to look at a flower with your whole being, or to be completely aware of the ways of your own mind. If you have done that, you will know with what clarity total attention brings into focus any problem. But to give such attention to anything is not easy, because our minds are very respectable; they are crippled with words and symbols, with ideas about what should be and what should not be.

I am talking about attention, and I wonder if you are paying attention, not just to what is being said, because that is of secondary importance, but are you attentive in the sense of being fully aware of the impediments, the blockages that your mind has created for itself? If you can be aware of these bondages—just be aware of them, without saying, 'What shall I do about them?'—you will find that they begin to break up; and then comes a state of attention in which there is no choice, no wandering off, because there is no longer a centre from which to wander. That state of attention is goodness; it is the only virtue. There is no other virtue.

So we realize that our minds are very limited. We have reduced the earth and the heavens, the vast movement of life, to a little corner called the 'me', the self, with its everlasting struggle to be or not to be. In what way can this mind, which is so small, so petty, so self-centred, break through the frontiers, the limitations that it has placed upon itself? As I said, it is only through attention, in which there is no choice, that the truth is seen; and it is truth that breaks the bondage, that sweeps away the limitations, not your effort, not your meditation, not your practices, your disciplines, your controls.

To be in this state of attention requires, surely, a knowledge of the 'me' and its ways. I must know myself; my mind must know the movement of every emotion, every thought. But knowledge is a peculiar thing. Knowledge is cumulative; it is ever in the past. In the present there is only knowing. Knowledge always colours knowing. We are concerned with knowing and not with knowledge, because knowledge about oneself distorts the knowing of oneself. I think there is a difference between knowing myself all the time and knowledge about myself. When self-knowledge is an accumulation of information that I have gathered about myself, it prevents the understanding of myself.

Look, the self, the 'me', is restless; it is always wandering, never still. It is like a roaring river, making a tremendous noise as it rushes down the valley. It is a living, moving thing; and how can one have knowledge about something that is constantly changing, never the same? The self is always in movement; it is never still, never quiet for a moment. When the mind has observed it, it is already gone. I do not know if you have ever tried to look at yourself, to pin down your mind to any one thing. If you do that, the thing you have pinned down is constantly before you, and so you have come to the end of self-knowledge. Am I conveying something?

Knowledge is always destructive to knowing. The knowing of oneself is never cumulative; it does not culminate in a point from which you judge the fact of what is the 'me'. You see, we accumulate knowledge, and from there we judge, and that is our difficulty. Having accumulated knowledge through experience, through learning, through reading, from that background we think, we function. We take up a position in knowledge, and from there we say, 'I know all about the self. It is greedy, stupid, everlastingly wanting to be superior'. The moment you take up a position in knowledge, your knowledge is very superficial. But if there is no accumulation of knowledge upon which the mind rests, then there is only the movement of knowing, and then the mind becomes extraordinarily swift in its perceptions.

So it is self-knowing that is important, and not self-knowledge. Knowing the movement of thought, knowing the movement of feeling without accumulation—and therefore with never a moment of judgment, of condemnation—is very important, because the moment there is accumulation, there is a thinker. The accumulation of knowledge gives a position to the mind, a centre from which to think; it gives rise to an observer who judges, condemns, identifies. But when there is self-knowing, there is neither the observer nor the observed; there is only a state of attention, of watching, learning.

Surely a mind that has accumulated knowledge can never learn. If the mind is to learn, it must not have the burden of knowledge, the burden of what it has accumulated. It must be fresh, innocent, free of the past. The accumulation of knowledge gives birth to the 'me'; but knowing can never do that because knowing is learning, and a mind that is constantly learning can have no resting place. If you really perceive the truth of this, not tomorrow but now, then you will find there is only a state of attention, of learning with never a moment of accumulation, and then the problems that most of us now have are completely gone. But this is not a trick by which to resolve your problems, nor is it a lesson for you to learn.

You see, a society such as ours—whether Indian, Russian, American, or what you will—is acquisitive, not only in the pursuit of material things but also in terms of competing, gaining, arriving, fulfilling. This society has so shaped our ways of thinking that we cannot free ourselves from the concept of a goal, an end. We are always thinking in terms of getting somewhere, of achieving inward peace, and so on. Our approach is always acquisitive. Physically we have to acquire to some extent; we must obviously provide ourselves with food, clothing, and shelter. But the mind uses these things as a means of further acquisition. I am talking about acquisition in the psychological sense. Just as the mind makes use of the physical necessities to acquire prestige and power, so through knowledge it establishes itself in a position of psychological certainty. Knowledge gives us a sense of security, does it not? From our background of experience, of accumulated knowledge about ourselves, we think and live, and this process creates a state of duality: what I am, and what I think I should be. There is therefore a contradiction, a constant battle between the two. But if one observes this process comprehensively, if one understands it, really feels its significance, then one will find that the mind is spontaneously good, alert, loving; it is always learning and never acquiring. Then self-knowledge has quite a different meaning, for it is no longer an accumulation of knowledge about oneself. Knowledge about oneself is small, petty, limiting, but knowing oneself is infinite; there is no end to it. So our problem is to abandon the ways of habit, of custom, of tradition, on the instant, and to be born anew.

One of our difficulties in all this is the problem of communion, or communication. I want to tell you something, and in the very telling it is perverted by the expression, the word that is used. What I would like to communicate to you, or to commune with you about, is very simple: total self-abandonment on the instant. That is all—not what happens after self-abandonment or the system that will bring it about. There is no system, because the moment you practise a system, you are obviously strengthening the self. Cannot the mind suddenly drop the anchors it has put down into the various patterns of existence?

Some evening when the sun was just going down, when the green rice fields were sparkling, when there was a lone passer-by and the birds were on the wing, it must have happened to you that there was all at once an extraordinary peace in the world. There was no 'you' watching, feeling, thinking, for you were that beauty, that peace, that infinite state of being. Such a thing must have happened to you if you have ever looked into the face of the world, into the vastness of the sky. How does it happen? When suddenly there is no worry, when you are no longer thinking that you love someone, or wondering if someone loves you, and you are in that state of love, that state of beauty, what has happened? The green tree, the blue sky, the dancing waters of the sea, the whole beauty of the earth—all this has driven out the ugly, petty little self, and for an instant you are all that. This is surely the state of self-abandonment without calculation.

To feel this sense of abandonment, you need passion. You cannot be sensitive if you are not passionate. Do not be afraid of that word *passion*. Most religious books, most gurus, swamis, leaders, say 'Don't have passion'. But if you have no passion, how can you be sensitive to the ugly, to the beautiful, to the whispering leaves, to the sunset, to a smile, to a cry? How can you be sensitive without a sense of passion in which there is abandonment? Do not ask how to acquire passion. People are passionate enough in getting a good job, or hating some poor chap, or being jealous of someone, but I am talking of something entirely different—a passion that *loves*. Love is a state in which there is no 'me'. Love is a state in which there is no condemnation, no saying that sex is right or wrong, that this is good and something else is bad. Love is none of these contradictory things. Contradiction does not exist in love. And how can one love if one is not passionate? Without passion, how can one be sensitive? To be sensitive is to feel your neighbour sitting next to you; it is to see the ugliness of the town with its squalor, its filth, its poverty, and to see the beauty of the river, the sea, the sky. If you are not passionate, how can you be sensitive to all that? How can you feel a smile, a tear? Love, I assure you, is passion. And without love, do what you will—follow this guru or that, read all the sacred books, become the greatest reformer, study Marx and have a revolution—it will be of no value, because when the heart is empty, without passion, without this extraordinary simplicity, there can be no self-abandonment.

Surely, the mind has abandoned itself and its moorings only when there is no desire for security. A mind that is seeking security can never know what love is. Self-abandonment is not the state of the devotee before his idol or his mental image. What we are talking about is as different from that as light is from darkness. Self-abandonment can come about only when you do not cultivate it and when there is self-knowing. Do please listen and feel your way into this.

When the mind has understood the significance of knowledge, only then is there self-knowing, and self-knowing implies self-abandonment. You have ceased to rest on any experience as a centre from which to observe, to judge, to weigh; therefore the mind has already plunged into the movement of self-abandonment. In that abandonment there is sensitivity. But the mind that is enclosed in its habits of eating, of thinking, in its habit of never looking at anything, such a mind obviously cannot be sensitive, cannot be loving. In the very abandonment of its own limitations, the mind becomes sensitive and therefore innocent. And only the innocent mind knows what love is, not the calculating mind, not the mind that has divided love into the carnal and the spiritual. In that state there is passion, and without passion reality will not come near you. It is only the enfeebled mind that invites reality, it is only the dull, grasping mind that pursues truth, God. But the mind that knows passion in love, to such a mind the nameless comes.

From Krishnamurti's Notebook, *Paris, September 1961*

September 21

THE EVENING LIGHT was on the river and the traffic across the bridge was furious and fast. The pavement was crowded with people returning home after a day's work in offices. The river was sparkling; there were ripples, small ones pursuing each other, with such delight. You could almost hear them, but the fury of the traffic was too much. Further down the river the light on the water was changing, becoming more deep, and it would soon be dark. The moon was on the other side of the huge tower, looking so out of place, so artificial; it had no reality, but the high steel tower had; there were people on it; the restaurant up there was lit up, and you could see crowds of people going into it. And as the night was hazy, the beams of the revolving lights were far stronger than the moon. Everything seemed so far away except the tower. How little we know about ourselves. We seem to know so much about other things, the distance to the moon, the atmosphere of Venus, how to put together the most extraordinary and complicated electronic brains, to break up the atoms and the minutest particle of matter. But we know so little about ourselves. To go to the moon is far more exciting than to go into ourselves; perhaps one's lazy or

frightened, or it's not profitable, in the sense of money and success, to go into ourselves. It's a much longer journey than to go to
the moon; no machines are available to take this journey, and no
one can help, no book, no theories, no guide. You have to do it
yourself. You have to have much more energy than in inventing
and putting together parts of a vast machine. You cannot get this
energy through any drug, through any interaction of relationship,
nor through control, denial. No gods, rituals, beliefs, prayers can
give it to you. On the contrary, in the very act of putting these
aside, in being aware of their significance, that energy comes to
penetrate into consciousness and beyond.

You can't buy that energy through accumulating knowledge about yourself. Every form of accumulation and the attach-
ment to it diminishes and perverts that energy. Knowledge about
yourself binds, weighs, ties you down; there's no freedom to move,
and you act and move within the limits of that knowledge. Learning
about yourself is never the same as accumulating knowledge about
yourself. Learning is active present, and knowledge is the past; if
you are learning in order to accumulate, it ceases to be learning.
Knowledge is static, because more can be added to it or taken away
from it, but learning is active—nothing can be added or taken away
from it for there is no accumulation at any time. Knowing, learning
about yourself has no beginning and no end, whereas knowledge
has. Knowledge is finite, and learning, knowing, is infinite.

You are the accumulated result of the many thousand
centuries of man, his hopes and desires, his guilts and anxieties,
his beliefs and gods, his fulfilments and frustrations; you are all
that and more additions made to it in recent times. Learning
about all this, deep down and on the surface, is not mere verbal or
intellectual statements of the obvious, the conclusions. Learning
is the experiencing of these facts, emotionally and directly—to
come into contact with them not theoretically, verbally, but actually, like a hungry man.

Learning is not possible if there's a learner; the learner
is the accumulated, the past, the knowledge. There is a division

between the learner and the thing he is learning about, and so there is conflict between them. This conflict destroys, diminishes energy to learn, to pursue to the very end the total make-up of consciousness. Choice is conflict, and choice prevents seeing; condemnation, judgment also prevent seeing. When this fact is seen, understood, not verbally, theoretically, but actually seen as fact, then learning is a moment-to-moment affair. And there is no end to learning; learning is all important, not the failures, successes, and mistakes. There is only seeing and not the seer and the thing seen. Consciousness is limited; its very nature is restriction; it functions within the frame of its own existence, which is experience, knowledge, memory. Learning about this conditioning breaks down the frame; then thought and feeling have their limited function; they then cannot interfere with the wider and deeper issues of life. Where the self ends, with all its secret and open intrigues, its compulsive urges and demands, its joys and sorrows, there begins a movement of life that is beyond time and its bondage.

September 25

Meditation is the flowering of understanding. Understanding is not within the borders of time; time never brings understanding. Understanding is not a gradual process to be gathered little by little, with care and patience. Understanding is now or never; it is a destructive flash, not a tame affair; it is this shattering that one is afraid of, and so one avoids it, knowingly or unknowingly. Understanding may alter the course of one's life, the way of thought and action; it may be pleasant or not, but understanding is a danger to all relationship. But without understanding, sorrow will continue. Sorrow ends only through self-knowing, the awareness of every thought and feeling, every movement of the conscious and that which is hidden. Meditation is the understanding of consciousness, the hidden and the open, and of the movement that lies beyond all thought and feeling.

The specialist cannot perceive the whole; his heaven is what he specializes in, but his heaven is a petty affair of the brain, the heaven of religion or of the technician. Capacity, gift, is obviously detrimental, for it strengthens self-centredness; it is fragmentary and so breeds conflict. Capacity has significance only in the total perception of life that is in the field of the mind and not of the brain. Capacity and its function are within the limits of the brain and so become ruthless, indifferent to the total process of life. Capacity breeds pride, envy, and its fulfilment becomes all important, and so it brings about confusion, enmity, and sorrow; it has its meaning only in the total awareness of life. Life is not merely at one fragmentary level, bread, sex, prosperity, ambition; life is not fragmentary; when it's made to be, it becomes utterly a matter of despair and endless misery. Brain functions in specialization of the fragment, in self-isolating activities and within the limited field of time. It is incapable of seeing the whole of life; the brain is a part, however educated it be; it is not the whole. Mind alone sees the whole, and within the field of the mind is the brain; the brain cannot contain the mind, do what it will.

To see wholly, the brain has to be in a state of negation. Negation is not the opposite of the positive; all opposites are related within the fold of each other. Negation has no opposite. The brain has to be in a state of negation for total seeing; it must not interfere, with its evaluations and justifications, with its condemnations and defences. It has to be still, not made still by compulsion of any kind, for then it is a dead brain, merely imitating and conforming. When it is in a state of negation, it is choicelessly still. Only then is there total seeing. In this total seeing that is the quality of the mind, there is no seer, no observer, no experiencer; there's only seeing. The mind then is completely awake. In this fully wakened state, there is no observer and the observed; there is only light, clarity. The contradiction and conflict between the thinker and thought cease.

Sources and Acknowledgments

From the report of the first public talk at Madras, 22 October 1958, in volume XI of *The Collected Works of J. Krishnamurti*, copyright © 1991 Krishnamurti Foundation of America.

From the report of the fifth public talk in Bombay, 24 February 1957, in volume X of *The Collected Works of J. Krishnamurti*, copyright © 1991 Krishnamurti Foundation of America.

The Learned or the Wise? from *Commentaries on Living First Series*, copyright © 1956 Krishnamurti Writings, Inc.

From *Krishnamurti's Notebook*, copyright © 1976 Krishnamurti Foundation Trust, Ltd.

From the recording of the second public talk at Saanen, 19 July 1970, copyright © 1970/1994 Krishnamurti Foundation Trust, Ltd.

From the recording of the third public talk at Brockwood Park, 12 September 1970, copyright © 1970/1994 Krishnamurti Foundation Trust, Ltd.

From the recording of the first public talk at Saanen, 15 July 1973, copyright © 1973/1994 Krishnamurti Foundation Trust, Ltd.

From the recording of the second public dialogue at Brockwood Park, 6 September 1973, copyright © 1973/1994 Krishnamurti Foundation Trust, Ltd.

From the recording of the second public dialogue at Brockwood Park, 31 August 1978, copyright © 1978/1994 Krishnamurti Foundation Trust, Ltd.

From the recording of the fourth public talk at Ojai, 15 April 1979, copyright © 1979/1994 Krishnamurti Foundation Trust, Ltd.

From the report of the eleventh talk with students at Rajghat, 22 December 1952, in volume VII of *The Collected Works of J. Krishnamurti*, copyright © 1991 Krishnamurti Foundation of America.